I0410420

ISRAEL IMPERILED:
THREATS TO THE JEWISH STATE

JOINT HEARING

BEFORE THE

SUBCOMMITTEE ON TERRORISM, NONPROLIFERATION, AND TRADE

AND THE

SUBCOMMITTEE ON THE MIDDLE EAST AND NORTH AFRICA

OF THE

COMMITTEE ON FOREIGN AFFAIRS
HOUSE OF REPRESENTATIVES

ONE HUNDRED FOURTEENTH CONGRESS

SECOND SESSION

APRIL 19, 2016

Serial No. 114–156

Printed for the use of the Committee on Foreign Affairs

Available via the World Wide Web: http://www.foreignaffairs.house.gov/ or
http://www.gpo.gov/fdsys/

U.S. GOVERNMENT PUBLISHING OFFICE

99–849PDF   WASHINGTON : 2016

For sale by the Superintendent of Documents, U.S. Government Publishing Office
Internet: bookstore.gpo.gov   Phone: toll free (866) 512–1800; DC area (202) 512–1800
Fax: (202) 512–2104   Mail: Stop IDCC, Washington, DC 20402–0001

CONTENTS

ISRAEL IMPERILED: THREATS TO THE JEWISH STATE

TUESDAY, APRIL 19, 2016

HOUSE OF REPRESENTATIVES,
SUBCOMMITTEE ON TERRORISM, NONPROLIFERATION, AND TRADE
AND
SUBCOMMITTEE ON THE MIDDLE EAST AND NORTH AFRICA,
COMMITTEE ON FOREIGN AFFAIRS,
Washington, DC.

The subcommittee met, pursuant to notice, at 1 o'clock p.m., in room 2172 Rayburn House Office Building, Hon. Ted Poe (chairman of the subcommittee) presiding.

Mr. POE. Subcommittees will come to order. Without objection, all members may have 5 days to submit statements, questions and extraneous materials for the record subject to the length limitation in the rules.

At this time, I will recognize myself for an opening statement. If someone would grab the back door, I would appreciate it. Thank you.

The state of Israel has always been surrounded by threats since its existence—threats by nations and terror groups that hate Israel because it is a Jewish state.

The goal of these haters has been to eliminate the state of Israel, an aggression started as soon as Israel became an established state. Arab armies amassed on its borders to destroy it. But yet, Israel has continued to exist in the face of suicide bombers and terrorist onslaughts like no country in history.

Most recently, 16 people in a bus were wounded yesterday in a bus bombing in Jerusalem, reminiscent of the wave of Palestinian suicide bombings that claimed so many lives a decade ago.

In recent years, the threats to Israel have increased and become even more dangerous. The volatile situation in Syria and its transformation into a full blown terrorist haven directly threatens Israel's security.

Al-Qaeda's Syrian affiliate, the Nusra Front, has at times literally straddled the Syrian-Israeli border. ISIS, which is even more brutal than al-Qaeda, controls large parts of Syria. Lebanese Hezbollah is heavily involved in the fighting in Syria, securing its valuable arms transfer corridor from its sponsors of no other than Iran.

Iran has transferred game-changing weapons systems into Lebanon to arm this terrorist proxy including anti-ship cruise missiles and air defense systems and precision-guided surface-to-surface missiles.

Hezbollah already has an estimated 150,000 rockets and missiles in its stockpile. That's enough to rain down 1,500 rockets a day in Israel for over 2 months.

All of these weapons systems are aimed for Israel. Hezbollah is amassing valuable tactical experience in Syria. It's mastered the use of diverse weapons systems and working in coordination with Iran and the Russians.

Meanwhile, there is Gaza. Israeli officials now believe that Hamas has completely replenished its rocket supply that Israel destroyed in 2014. Hamas is building a sophisticated network of tunnels under the Gaza Strip for the purpose of securing arms supply lines and using those tunnels to strike at Israel.

Yesterday, Israeli officials announced the discovery of a Hamas tunnel running from Gaza into the Israeli territory fully equipped with electricity, communication lines and a rail line.

All of these actions by all of these groups and states are aggression against Israel. Israel tries to defend its sovereignty the best it can.

There's also a new kind of terrorism. Since September, Palestinian lone wolf terrorists have carried out hundreds of attacks against civilians in Israel. These terrorists will do anything to kill, stab, ram their vehicles into civilians and they just shoot indiscriminately.

They are field directed by the hateful incitement of the Palestinian Authority. Palestinian Authority President Abbas proclaimed, "We welcome every drop of blood spilled in Jerusalem. This is pure blood—blood on its way to Allah."

This latest wave of attacks has killed 34 people, injured over 400. Among those killed were two Americans, one of which is from my state of Texas, Taylor Force. He was an Eagle Scout, a West Point grad, and he served in Afghanistan and Iraq.

Aside from terrorism, Israel also faces a threat that also seeks its ultimate destruction. In recent years, the global boycott, divestment, and sanctions movement has led to an onslaught of campaigns targeting Israel.

This is—this movement, obviously, doesn't like the settlements in the West Bank. Settlements in the West Bank, in my opinion, are an internal matter for Israel and it is nobody else's business what a state decides on where people live and don't live. Out-of-towners, including the BDS and our own State Department, need to stay out of where people live in Israel. We certainly wouldn't like someone telling us where people should settle in the United States.

And then, of course, we have the nuclear Iran deal. The deal makes it only a matter of time before the mullahs in Tehran develop a nuclear weapon.

Given their anti-Semitic rhetoric, we all know what they intend to with that bomb. The $100 billion signing bonus and the financial boon expected with sanctions relief raise serious concern about the world's number-one state sponsor of terrorism. That's Iran.

They will funnel more and more cash to their terrorist groups all over the world. Reports since the deal went into effect indicate that both Iran significantly has increased its financial support for both terrorist groups, Hezbollah and Hamas.

In February, Iran announced that it would give $7,000 to families of Palestinians who kill Israelis, an additional $30,000 to every family whose home Israel demolished due to the family's involvement in terrorism.

Since the nuclear deal was struck, Iran has launched three ballistic missile tests. The most recent one launched missiles marked with the words ''Israel must be wiped off the map.''

The deal will lift the international ban on Iran's ballistic missiles in 8 years. It's no wonder why Israeli leaders call the joint comprehensive plan of action a bad deal for Israel's survival.

Despite these threats, our relationship with Israel has become strained under current administration policies. We must do more to repair this important relationship and protect our friends and allies.

We must make it clear that all of these actions against Israel are because it is a Jewish state. Israel and the United States share common values. We must recognize that the threats that confront Israel really affect the United States as well.

The same terrorist group that wants to destroy Israel first wants to destroy the United States. The United States must show that it is partnered with Israel in its self-defense, and Israel, in the meantime, better keep its powder dry, and that is just the way it is.

I will recognize the ranking member on the Terrorism Subcommittee, Mr. Keating from Massachusetts.

Mr. KEATING. Thank you, Chairman Poe, and thank you for conducting this hearing. I would also like to welcome and thank Chair Ros-Lehtinen, Ranking Member Deutch and members of the Middle East and North Africa Subcommittee for joining us today. Welcome.

Lastly, I'd like to thank our panel for being here to discuss the various threats to Israel. You're all experts in your field and I look forward to hearing the nuances you bring to this vital topic.

The United States and Israel have always had a special relationship. The relationship is unlike any other and it is founded on common values and shared interests and certainly all of us keep the people that were injured just recently in the bus bombing in our thoughts and prayers for their full recovery.

Our country has defended Israel's right to exist since the very beginning—a stance we have demonstrated through will and force. Historically, Israel is the top recipient of U.S. military aid and administration after administration has worked to ensure that Israel maintains its qualitative military edge.

We have witnessed continued funding for the Iron Dome defense system. We've doubled the stockpiles of emergency military equipment for Israel and, first, you know, we've approved the sale of bunker-busting bombs to Israel as well.

Additionally, we're in the process of creating a new memorandum of understanding which could ultimately increase the security assistance already provided to Israel.

This support is designed to deter and to mitigate threats to one of our closest allies, and as I'm confident my colleagues agree it's the role of the United States as a global leader, an active member of the United Nations, and as a friend of Israel to promote, encourage regional stability in the Middle East.

Like many other countries in the region, Israel faces a number of challenges to its security both internally and externally.

Externally, the Islamic State is active in both countries northern and southern boundaries, and Israel continues to face a constant threat from Hezbollah.

Internally, violence between Israelis and Palestinians highlights this systemic distrust between the two groups. The prospects for renewed peace talks are low.

Going forward, it is imperative we remain an honest and effective broker in assisting Israel in its security needs as well as promoting our own foreign policy goals in the region. This includes at times carefully examining Israel's actions to ensure they remain in line and consistent with our own American values and interests.

As I said at the beginning, there are nuances to these topics and areas that need to be objectively examined. I hope we can hear today about the various challenges Israel faces not just from terrorist organizations but also economic pressures through the BDS movement.

But most importantly, I would like to hear how the U.S. and Israel can cooperate to solve these challenges, and I yield back, Mr. Chairman.

Mr. POE. I thank the gentleman from Massachusetts.

The Chair recognizes the chairman of the Middle East and North Africa Subcommittee, Ms. Ileana Ros-Lehtinen from Florida.

Ms. ROS-LEHTINEN. Thank you so much, Judge Poe, and I am so glad that both of our subcommittees have called this hearing jointly to discuss the many threats that Israel faces.

Unfortunately, as both of our speakers have pointed out, this hearing is quite timely. Israel fell victim to a disgusting terror attack as 21 people were injured in a bus bombing in Jerusalem just yesterday.

Our thoughts and prayers are with the victims and the families and the people of Israel as they continue to seek peace and security.

These so-called lone wolf attacks and knife-wielding individuals are said to be more difficult to protect against because there is no real organization or planning for it—just folks who are being incited to conduct these types of vicious attacks.

It's the message they receive from the Palestinian leadership and Abu Mazen and this is where the U.S. can do more. We can have more of an impact because Israel clearly knows how to best protect her citizens. But the Obama administration should be using the leverage we have over the Palestinian Authority to press it to stop the incitement and work with Israel to promote peace.

However, the terrorist threats that Israel faces aren't just limited to these bus bombings or knife attacks. I convened a hearing of our subcommittee last month on the growing threat that Hezbollah presents for Israel, and thanks to the Iran nuclear deal the Obama administration negotiated, Hezbollah stands to get even more financial and material support from Tehran.

Even as Hezbollah fights in Syria, Iran has been transferring advanced weapons and weapons systems to its proxies through Syria and to Lebanon.

Estimates now place Hezbollah's missile and rocket stockpiles in the area of 150,000. That is more than ten times the amount when it indiscriminately rained down over 100 rockets a day for 32 days at northern Israel in the year 2006 and this number now includes more sophisticated missiles with guidance systems, putting Israel at even greater risk.

Hamas remains a constant threat and in fact, as Judge Poe mentioned, Israel recently just discovered the first Hamas tunnel from Gaza that reaches into Israel since the 2014 fighting.

And though Egypt may help destroy some of Hamas' tunnels, much more assistance is needed in the fight in the Sinai against terror groups there including ISIS and al-Qaeda affiliates.

These terror groups are near Israel's borders in the Golan Heights and in Syria and in Sinai and are trying to gain more influence within the Palestinian territories as well.

If Iran is the number-one threat facing Israel—threat 1A is Hezbollah, Hamas and all of the terror groups just on its borders—then threat 1B has to be the ongoing efforts by Abu Mazen and the Palestinian leadership to delegitimize and isolate Israel on the international stage at the U.N. and other similar efforts like a boycott, divest, and sanctions—BDS—movement.

It is no secret that Abu Mazen has been pushing his scheme for unilateral statehood at the U.N., trying to circumvent the peace process and a direct negotiated settlement with the Israelis.

This effort saw UNESCO admit the nonexistent state of Palestine to its membership and then shortly after saw the U.N. upgrade the Palestinian status to nonmember observer status.

Of course, we all know that UNESCO, the U.N. Human Rights Council, and the U.N. in general have an anti-Israel agenda. Just in the past few weeks, we saw the Human Rights Council vote to establish a black list of companies that could be used by those seeking to participate in BDS and which gives the impression that the U.N. supports BDS.

UNESCO once again moved to remove any Jewish historical ties to Jerusalem and we know that the Palestinians are working to reintroduce resolutions at the U.N. Security Council that would impose a two-state solution on Israel along with artificial time lines for negotiations.

I have asked the administration on several occasions to clarify its position on Israel at the U.N. Security Council but we never get a straight answer, Mr. Chairman.

It should be simple. It has been longstanding U.S. policy to veto any such resolution as we have in the past and as the Palestinians are seeking to support—seeking support for now. Yet, the administration will not reaffirm that policy.

This is worrisome and we should continue to press the administration to do more to stand by Israel and make it clear in no uncertain terms that we will veto any resolution that imposes a solution upon Israel.

6

We need to also take a closer look at all of those behind the BDS movement and work to counter these efforts. Thank you so much, Mr. Chairman, for this joint hearing.

Mr. POE. I thank the gentlelady.

The Chair recognizes the gentleman from Florida, Mr. Deutch, for his opening statement—the ranking member of the subcommittee.

Mr. CONNOLLY. Thank you very much. Thank you, Chairman Poe and Chairman Ros-Lehtinen, for holding today's hearing, and thank you to my fellow ranking member, Ranking Member Keating, and thanks to all of you for your strong support of the U.S.-Israel relationship.

I'd like to echo the sentiments of my colleagues in expressing my deep sympathy for the individuals injured in the bus bombing on Monday and to their families.

This atrocious attack is unacceptable and unfortunately is emblematic of the constant threats that Israel faces. The hearing today gives us the opportunity to assess the very dangers facing Israel.

To fully understand these threats and their effects on the U.S.-Israel relationship, we have to take a serious look at all of the challenges Israel faces on a daily basis, both strategic and political.

Our two governments are currently in negotiations over a new 10-year memorandum of understanding that will serve as the basis of our assistance relationship.

The United States has never wavered on its commitment to ensuring Israel is able to defend herself against any and all threats and a new MOU must reflect the current and future security threats to Israel for both state and nonstate actors.

At any given time Israel faces the threat of rocket attacks from every single corner of her territory, from Hezbollah missiles shot from Lebanon, Syria to the north, Hamas rockets from the south, ISIS-affiliated militants Sinai.

Hezbollah, a terrorist organization founded on the premise of resistance to the Zionist regime and bankrolled by Iran, now has an arsenal of over 150,000 rockets, many with advanced capabilities.

Hezbollah's 6,000 to 8,000 mercenaries are fighting in the Syrian conflict and have been given access to even more advanced weaponry. Weapons flown from Iran to Hezbollah via Syria are being placed in precarious locations close to Israel's border, in the Golan Heights, for example.

And last week, Prime Minister Netanyahu publically acknowledged that Israel has had to strike down dozens of these kind of convoys in order to prevent Hezbollah from stockpiling what he referred to as game-changing weapons on Israel's borders.

Operating out of Gaza, Hamas and Palestinian Islamic jihad, two more of Iran's beneficiaries, have carried out decades of violent attacks on Israeli civilians. During the 50 days of Operation Protective Edge in 2014, 4,564 rockets and mortars were fired at Israel from Gaza. But thanks to the robust cooperative missile defense programs between the United States and Israel, Iron Dome was able to intercept over 700 rockets that would have landed in populated areas.

Since September 2015, Israelis faced a new wave of violence, this time in the form of what have been dubbed lone wolf attacks. These deadly stabbings, shootings and car rammings aren't coming from lone terrorists or those affiliated with terror cells.

Instead, these attackers are using kitchen knives, axes and their vehicles to target random Israeli citizens. These lone wolf attacks have taken the lives of over 30 people including American students Ezra Schwartz and Taylor Force.

These attacks are the result of, among others, the violent incitement within Palestinian society and I was proud to join Chairman Ros-Lehtinen in offering a resolution that passed the House unanimously last fall condemning incitement within the Palestinian Authority.

The entire world must condemn these indiscriminate attacks. Of course, Iran continues to pose an existential threat to Israel despite concluding the nuclear agreement. In an outrageous display of defiance, Iran recently test fired a ballistic missile emblazoned with the phrase ''Israel must be wiped off the Earth'' in Hebrew.

Many of us, both supporters and opponents of the nuclear deal, are deeply committed to ensuring that the funds gained from sanctions relief do not go toward supporting terrorism aimed at Israel or others in the region.

This includes funding and exporting weapons to terrorist organizations. It includes the continued development of ballistic missiles capable of delivering a nuclear warhead, and it includes attempts to stir up trouble in other countries in the Middle East in an attempt to provoke instability across the region.

And there is nothing in the Iran nuclear deal—there is nothing in the deal that prevents additional sanctions from being imposed against Iran for those areas outside of the nuclear deal including their support for terrorism, nor is there anything in the nuclear deal that prevents states like my own state of Florida from continuing to ensure that our state pension money and all those funds do not contribute to Iran's destabilizing activities in the region.

And not all the threats facing Israel are security related. In the past year, the supporters of boycott, divestment and sanctions—the economic warfare against Israel—disturbingly gained traction as they positioned themselves as a means of nonviolent resistance.

In reality, what they're doing is unjustly singling out and demonizing one country—Israel. And I wish the voices of those who support BDS spoke out against the dozens of tyrannical regimes who violate the human rights of their people every day. And while it's perfectly acceptable for people to criticize government policies, it is unacceptable when that criticism is intended to attack the legitimacy and the very existence of a nation, and that is what the BDS movement does.

Unfortunately, those hurt most by BDS efforts often are Palestinian workers whose jobs are put at risk by those who seek to boycott Israel. We have to work toward the goal of a two-state solution—two states living side by side in peace and security with thriving economies—and the BDS movement only pushes the prospects of peace further out of reach by unjustly placing blame on one side instead of urging both sides to the negotiating table.

And finally, Mr. Chairman, while efforts—and Madam Chairman—while efforts to delegitimize Israel in the international community are nothing new, Israel and their allies must continue to meet them with resolve.

The United Nations Human Rights Council continues to debate and pass anti-Israel resolutions at every one of its meetings while ignoring Syria, Iran, and the rest of the world's human rights abusers.

These efforts must be condemned and, further, any effort that seeks to circumvent direct negotiations between Israel and the Palestinians must be opposed. The only path to two states for two peoples is through direct negotiations between the two parties.

This should be encouraged by anyone who considers themselves to be a friend of Israel and by anyone who claims to want what's best for the Palestinian people.

We have to recognize U.S. and Israel stand together not just because we share security concerns but because we share the same values of democracy, equality, and freedom; and I look forward to discussing the ways in which we can keep Israel vibrant and strong, protect the security of our ally, and foster an environment that is conducive to peace.

And I appreciate the time, Mr. Chairman.

Mr. POE. Appreciate the comments by the gentleman from Florida.

The Chair will now recognize other members for a 1-minute opening statement if they wish. I'm going to ask the members to keep it to 1 minute or less so we can get our witnesses—have them testify and try to do all of this before we have to break for votes.

The Chair recognizes the gentleman from South Carolina, Mr. Wilson, for 1 minute.

Mr. WILSON. Thank you, Chairman Ted Poe and Chairwoman Ileana Ros-Lehtinen, for holding this important joint hearing with distinguished witnesses.

As our closest ally in the Middle East, Israel faces some of the greatest threats in its history. Most critically, the bizarre Iran nuclear deal has provided the Iranian regime over $100 billion—enabling them the further promote terrorism, which enhances threats to Israel.

Even more dangerously, the deal provides for Iranian regime to provide a path forward to producing nuclear weapons. This fact, combined with Iran's testing of two ballistic missiles, in March reveals a clear picture of damage that the President's short-sighted deal could potentially have on American families.

To make matters worse, these two ballistic missiles included the phrase, ''Israel must be wiped off the map,'' written in Hebrew as a blatant threat.

Aside from the threat of Iran, Israel has suffered from an increase in lone wolf terrorist attacks. According to Israeli intelligence, there have been more than 230 attacks in the last 7 months, killing 34 persons, injuring 400.

I look forward to the bipartisan cooperation that we have already heard today, working with our colleagues. I yield back.

Mr. POE. The Chair recognizes the gentleman from Virginia, Mr. Connolly. The Chair recognizes Mr. Connolly if he wants to give an opening statement—from Virginia.

Mr. CONNOLLY. Thank you, Mr. Chairman.

I echo the concerns of my colleagues about the security of Israel and the lack of balance at international institutions including the United Nations when examining human rights violations and policies that subjugate whole parts of a population.

I also think, candidly, that a threat to Israel is also internal and we ought to be examining that as well as a friend to Israel—the concern—the long-term concern of the consequences of an endless occupation of the West Bank and the demographic imperative of the growth of both an Arab and Palestinian population.

These are our concerns to deep friends of Israel and certainly we heard some of those echoed by the Vice President of the United States last night.

In any event, I'm glad we're having a hearing and I hope we look at both and I want to certainly associate myself with the remarks of Mr. Deutch. At the end of the day, there could be no substitute for the two parties sitting down and having direct talks if we're ever going to have peace in this corner of the world.

I thank the chair.

Mr. POE. The Chair recognizes the gentleman from Florida, Mr. DeSantis.

Mr. DESANTIS. Thank you, Mr. Chairman. Thanks for having this hearing. I support Prime Minister Netanyahu's declaration that the Golan Heights should not be given back to Syria. I think that would attract terrorists. They'd be launching attacks against the Jewish state incessantly.

We've seen the Iran deal has really hastened Iran's ascent as the dominant Islamist power in the region. They are firing missiles. They're exporting terrorism. They have a major cash influx.

We're told that Israel needs to make all these concessions for peace with the Palestinians but the Palestinians still don't recognize Israel's right to exist as a Jewish state and still incite terrorism and hatred against the Jewish people.

Our friends in Europe sometimes don't fare much better. Many of those countries are moving in the direction of boycotting Israel, the only democracy in the Middle East, and they hold no other country to that same standard.

So I appreciate your holding this hearing. I think we have to take these threats to Israel seriously and I look forward to a new administration coming in and finally moving our Embassy to Jerusalem where it belongs.

Thank you. I yield back.

Mr. POE. I thank the gentleman.

The Chair recognizes the gentleman from Rhode Island, Mr. Cicilline, for his 1-minute opening statement.

Mr. CICILLINE. Thank you, Chairman Poe, Chairman Ros-Lehtinen, Ranking Members Keating and Deutch for calling this hearing on the threats to the Jewish state.

With the rise of violence within Israel and the growing instability in the region at large this hearing is very timely. I'd also like to thank our witnesses for being here today.

Like others, I'd like to express my horror and outrage at yesterday's terrorist attack of Jerusalem that targeted innocent men, women and children. My thoughts and prayers are with the victims of this horrific attack and their families.

It is completely unacceptable that the Israeli people continue to live under the constant threat of terrorist violence. I know my colleague has joined me in strong support of the people of Israel today.

We will do everything we can to help bring those responsible to justice and provide whatever assistance is necessary to combat the threat of terrorism. Israel, like every nation, has the right to protect its people against cowardly terrorist attacks.

The fact that this violence has escalated over the past 2 years is especially troubling and the fact that the Palestinian Authority has not taken a forceful stance against this terrorism threatens the long-term stability of both the Israelis and the Palestinians and threatens peace negotiations going forward.

Both sides must do all they can to foster an environment for seeking peace, and the United States must continue to be there to encourage both sides to seek peace and to ensure Israel's security.

This hearing will help us better understand all the threats facing Israel in the rapidly changing and dangerous context of these threats.

I look forward to hearing from the witnesses and I thank you, Mr. Chairman, and yield back.

Mr. POE. The Chair recognizes Mr. Trott for his opening statement.

Mr. TROTT. I'd like to thank our respective committee chairs and ranking members for holding this important hearing.

As has been mentioned several times already, Israel is under constant threat from Iran and their proxies—a threat that's intensified under the administration's repeated acquiescence.

I was an early and often outspoken critic of the nuclear deal with Iran, and if you look at their behavior over the past 6 months it's pretty clear that my comments were correct, and I continue to maintain you can't do a good deal with a bad guy.

Most recently, it was rumored that the administration was looking to do an end around Congress and give Iran access to the U.S. dollar—yet another concession.

In an effort to stop this misguided policy, I recently introduced legislation that would block the Department of Treasury from providing Iran access to the U.S. dollar. If the administration is not willing to stand with Israel then it's even more important to show the world that the House of Representatives will.

Thank you, and I yield back.

Mr. POE. I thank the gentleman.

Now that we have all had our say, you will get your say but not so quick. We are now in the middle of votes. We will return after votes, and then we will hear from our witnesses.

Thank you for your patience. So the committees stand adjourned until 10 minutes after votes are concluded.

[Recess.]

Mr. POE. The subcommittees will come to order.

Without objection, all of the witnesses' prepared statements will be made part of the record. I ask that each witness keep your presentation to no more than 5 minutes. When the red light comes on that means stop talking.

I'll introduce each witness and then give them time for opening statements. Dr. Michael Rubin is currently a resident scholar at the American Enterprise Institute where he focuses on terrorism.

He formally served as a Pentagon official whose major research areas were the Middle East, Turkey, Iran and diplomacy.

Dr. Jonathan Schanzer is the vice president and researcher at the Foundation for Defense of Democracies where he focuses on Palestinian politics, Iran, and Israeli affairs. He previously served as terrorism finance analyst at the U.S. Department of Treasury.

Mr. David Makovsky is the Ziegler distinguished fellow with the Irwin Levy Foundation Program on the U.S.-Israel Strategic Relationship at the Washington Institute for Near East Policy.

He recently served as a senior advisor on Secretary Kerry's Middle East peace team.

Dr. Tamara Cofman Wittes is the director of the Center for Middle East Policy at the Brookings Institute. She previously served as deputy assistant director of secretary of the state for Near Eastern Affairs, coordinating U.S. policy on democracy and human rights in the Middle East.

Dr. Rubin, we'll start with you.

STATEMENT OF MICHAEL RUBIN, PH.D., RESIDENT SCHOLAR, AMERICAN ENTERPRISE INSTITUTE

Mr. RUBIN. Chairman Poe, Ranking Member Keating, Chairman Ros-Lehtinen, Ranking Member Deutch, distinguished representatives, it is an honor to speak before you today about the growing threats Israel faces to its security.

I have detailed in my written testimony how Iran's Islamic Revolutionary Guard Corps will benefit disproportionately from Iran's reintegration into the world economy.

Because the IRGC cares far less about bolstering the prosperity of Iranian citizenry versus resourcing its ideological desire to undermine, delegitimize, and attack Israel, Israel faces enhanced enemy capabilities on almost all fronts.

I do not want to repeat the threats described by my fellow panelists in their written testimony. All these are relevant and true. Rather, I would like to draw attention to two looming problems that are not receiving adequate attention.

In recent years, Iran has developed a number of different surveillance and attack drones. While its claims to have reverse engineered a downed CIA drone are risible, U.S. military pilots flying over the Persian Gulf regularly describe seeing Iranian UAVs.

Iran has openly deployed its indigenous UAV technology into Syria and Iraq and perhaps Lebanon as well. Iranian UAVs fly over Syria's largest city in Aleppo and so could just as easily fly over the Golan Heights, the Galilee, or into international air paths over Tel Aviv, Ben Gurion International Airport, or Israel's smaller regional airports.

That Iranian sources openly brag about their development to both suicide drones and new satellite-guided drone navigation capabilities augments concern.

Neither Iran nor its proxies need to be able to strike an aircraft or an airport to be successful. Simply interfering with civilian air traffic will likely augment Israel's isolation as airlines suspend service into Tel Aviv.

Nor is the UAV threat the only one looming for Israel. With the discovery of gas fields in eastern Mediterranean, Lebanese authorities have asserted a claim to 300 square miles of Israeli waters.

Therefore, even though the United Nations formally certified Israel's withdrawal from Lebanon complete, the dispute over Shebaa Farms notwithstanding, Lebanon has resurrected a new claim that provides Hezbollah cover to pursue its rearmament and terrorism.

Indeed, Hezbollah has bragged that it has been training operatives in underwater sabotage. This not only suggests a new terror capability that could be utilized against Israel but is also a direct threat to many American engineers and oil workers involved in the region.

As we consider the threats not only to Israel but the United States and our moderate Arab allies as well, it is essential to consider not only the enhancement of terrorist missile threats Israel has long faced but also the new platforms which will be used to attack the Jewish state.

Since Israel's enemies make no secret of their desire also to target and defeat the United States, it is time to begin a serious discussion about how to reformulate Israel's qualitative military edge for the next generation.

I also want to just add one separate point with regard to the demographic imperative and the demographic challenges which Israel faced.

We should not be distracted by notions of the demographic imperative as oftentimes we are now. The Palestinian Statistics Agency's statistics cannot be taken at face value.

They double count Jerusalem, they refuse to count emigration, and if you compare multiple censes you notice that the predications are off by several percentage points and are, frankly, readjusted with magic numbers.

Bad data, even if diplomatically convenient, oftentimes leads to bad policy, and with that, I conclude.

Thank you very much.

[The prepared statement of Mr. Rubin follows:]

American Enterprise Institute
for Public Policy Research

Statement before the House Foreign Affairs Committee

Joint Hearing on "Israel Imperiled: Threats to the Jewish State"

Subcommittee on Terrorism, Nonproliferation, and Trade
Subcommittee on the Middle East and North Africa

"New Directions in the Iranian and Hezbollah Threat against Israel

Michael Rubin
Resident Scholar
American Enterprise Institute

April 19, 2016

Chairman Poe, Ranking Member Keating; Chairman Ros-Lehtinen, Ranking Member Deutch, distinguished representatives, it is an honor to speak before you today about the growing threats Israel faces to its security.

Israel and, for that matter, moderate Arab states across the Middle East as well, face a growing threat from a resurgent Islamic Republic of Iran. The Joint Comprehensive Plan of Action (JCPOA) has been a game changer, but not necessarily in the way the Obama administration recognizes.

To claim a decade-long deal to be a success is disingenuous simply because the JCPOA front-loaded tens of billions of dollars in unfrozen assets, sanctions relief, and new investment. On one hand, if Tehran walks away from its commitment, it will have pocketed more than 20 times the annual budget of the Islamic Revolutionary Guard Corps. On the other hand, if Iran fully complies with the JCPOA, it will be left in little more than a decade with an industrial scale nuclear program greater than that which Pakistan possessed when it built itself a nuclear arsenal.

In the near term, Israel and other regional states must face the empowerment not only of the Islamic Revolutionary Guard Corps, but also its terrorist proxies. Just over a year ago, Acting State Department Spokesman Marie Harf insisted the Iranian government would use its perhaps $50 billion or more windfall to repair its own economy rather than invest in further terror.[1] This belief, however, reflects ignorance over both the ideology of the Islamic Republic and the structure of the Iranian economy.

"Export of Revolution"
A consistent problem with U.S. diplomacy toward Iran has been the projection by senior American officials of U.S. values and models upon the Islamic Republic. Successive proponents of engagement have embraced the notion that the Iranian government wishes to resolve conflict and become a normal, status quo power. They believe, therefore, that their Iranian counterparts—President Hassan Rouhani or Foreign Minister Mohammad Javad Zarif, for example, are sincere in their desire for peace and reconciliation and motivated by a desire for prosperity.

Alas, this ignores the Iranian concern of "export of revolution," enshrined not only in the Islamic Republic's constitution as its *raison d'être*, but also in the founding Statute of the Islamic Revolutionary Guard Corps (IRGC). Article 3 of Iran's Constitution declares the goals of the regime to be both "the expansion and strengthening of Islamic brotherhood and public cooperation among all the people" and "unsparing support to the oppressed of the world," while Article 154 calls for "support of the just struggles of the oppressed against the arrogant in every corner of the globe." This was not mere social justice. Revolutionary Leader Ayatollah Ruhollah Khomeini,

---

[1] Marie Harf. "State Department Daily Briefing." April 17, 2015.

leader of the Iranian Revolution, defined the repressed as any living under a system other than Iran's. "The United States can't do a damned thing; we will export our revolution to the world," became Khomeini's mantra and, subsequently, an IRGC slogan.[2]

On July 25, 1981, the IRGC monthly *Payam-e Enghelab* defined "the principle of jihad" as one of the two main tasks of the Guards, the other being defending the supreme leader's government. In the early years of the Islamic Revolution, Iran sought to export revolution to Lebanon, Saudi Arabia, Bahrain, Pakistan, Iraq, and others. With the exception of Lebanon, where Hezbollah took root, all Iran accomplished was bad blood between Tehran and regional capitals.

Still the acceptance of "export of revolution" has been a commonality between both Iranian government hard-liners and reformers. Initially, there was some debate, however, about what "export of revolution" meant. In a May 3, 2008, speech, former President Mohammad Khatami suggested that Iranian officials redefine the concept in terms of soft power. "What did the Imam want, and what was his purpose of exporting the revolution? Did he wish us to export revolution by means of gunpowder or groups sabotaging other countries?" Khatami asked, before suggesting Khomeini "meant to establish a role model here, which means people should see that in this society, the economy, science, and dignity of man are respected."[3] In effect, Khatami argued not against the existence of "export of revolution," but rather that the government could interpret it as soft power.

Government authorities, however, were furious. Not only had Khatami undercut Iran's plausible deniability by acknowledging state-sanctioned terror, but he also proposed diluting a pillar of the revolution. Seventy-seven members of parliament responded by demanding the Intelligence Ministry investigate Khatami for his comments.[4] As the controversy over Khatami's remarks faded, Ayatollah Mahmoud Hashemi Shahroudi, arguably the third most powerful cleric in Iran and the man whom Khamenei not only regularly uses as his stand-in but also whom Iranian officials seek to position to replace Grand Ayatollah Ali Sistani upon his death, reiterated Tehran's continued commitment to export the revolution through violence. Speaking to armed forces, he declared the IRGC to be "the hope of Islamic national and Islamic liberation movements."[5]

This is not mere theory. In the months since agreement was struck and the JCPOA came into effect, Iranian efforts to destabilize regional countries have accelerated. Bahraini authorities have intercepted assault rifles, explosives, and detonators which the IRGC apparently was seeking to

---

[2] "Tars-e Amrika az Ahiya-e Islami" [The US Fear of the Islamic Revival], trans Open Source Center, *Khorasan* (Mashhad), January 25, 1996; "Tandar bidun Baran" [Thunder without Rain], Javar (Tehran), August 18, 2005.
[3] "Khatami: Dar Zamineh-e tahrif andisheh-ha-ye hazirat-e Imam 'alam khatar mikonam" [Khatami: I Find Danger in the Distortion of His Excellence the Imam's Thoughts], Tehran Emrooz, May 3, 2008.
[4] "Jamayeh-i Avari Imza 'Alebeh Khatami" [Gathering Signatures against Khatami], *E'temad* (Tehran), May 7, 2008.
[5] "Iran's Forces Are Models of Resistance," Press TV (Tehran), May 22, 2008.

smuggle into Bahrain.[6] More recently, the U.S. Navy has intercepted Iranian weaponry destined for Yemeni rebels.[7] Iran's state-controlled press has openly featured recruitment drives to sign up students to fight in Syria.[8]

Reinforcing the Revolutionary Guard Economy

Even if the Iranian government were sincere in its desire to rejoin the international community as a normal state, it would likely not be able to change the behavior of the Islamic Revolutionary Guard Corps and other groups which directly promote and sponsor terrorism. Make no mistake: The primary if not only winner from the JCPOA has been the IRGC. This is because it maintains a stranglehold over trade and the economy and so has become the chief if not sole beneficiary from the hard currency now flowing into Iran. Here the problem is *Gharargah Sazandegi-ye Khatam al-Anbiya*, the IRGC's economic wing. To understand what Khatam al-Anbiya is, picture the U.S. Army Corps of Engineers combined with Bechtel, Halliburton, KBR, Shell, Exxon, Boeing, and Northrop-Grumman, all rolled up into one. Today, Khatam al-Anbiya monopolizes heavy industry, shipping, electronics, manufacturing as well as import-export. All together, it controls perhaps 40 percent of the Iranian economy.

While the official IRGC budget may only be $5 billion per year, the income the IRGC derives from smuggling across the Persian Gulf accounts for another $13 billion annually. Under former President Mahmoud Ahmadinejad, IRGC-linked companies received upwards of $50 billion in no-bid contracts in the oil industry alone. In short, even if President Hassan Rouhani were to take the IRGC's official budget to zero, it would be facing less of a budget cutback proportionately than the U.S. military has through sequestration.

To believe that tying Iran more directly into trade and the international economy promotes political liberalization is to ignore precedent. As demonstrated in my recent book, *Dancing with the Devil*, a history of a half century of diplomatic engagement with rogue regimes and terrorist groups, between 1998 and 2005, the European Union more than doubled its trade with Iran on the philosophy that trade and the promotion of economic liberalization might lead to political liberalization. At the same time, the price of oil—and the bulk of Iran's income—nearly quintupled. That cash infusion, alas, coincided with the collapse of the reform movement which largely ran out of steam by 2000. It also coincided with a massive infusion of cash into Iran's ballistic missile and nuclear programs and the construction of the then-covert enrichment plant at Natanz. This is why many Iranian reformists claim credit for advancing the nuclear program.

---

[6] "Bahrain disrupts attempt to smuggle explosives into Kingdom," Bahrain News Agency, July 25, 2015.
[7] Sam LaGrone, "U.S. Navy Seizes Suspected Iranian Arms Shipment Bound for Yemen," U.S. Naval Institute News, April 6 2016.
[8] "Nahaveh Sabatnam az Davtaliban Modafa' Haram" ("Registering Volunteers to Defend the Shrines,") *Shargh*, January 27, 2016.

Israel Faces a Renewed Terrorist Threat

In the wake of the 2006 war between Israel and Hezbollah, many diplomats and journalists argued that Hezbollah had effectively become a Lebanese nationalist organization and did not necessarily answer to Iran and the IRGC. While useful politically and diplomatically to exculpate Iran for Hezbollah terrorism, it is also untrue. While Hassan Nasrallah leads Hezbollah on a daily base as its secretary-general, Hezbollah continues to describe Ali Khamenei as its 'source of emulation.' In 2008, Hezbollah turned its guns on fellow Lebanese in the heart of Beirut as a result of a dispute over revenue sharing and control over Beirut's international airport. More recently, Hezbollah has operated effectively under the command of IRGC Qods Force chief Qassem Soleimani in Syria, a conflict in which those motivated by Lebanese nationalism should have no interest.

Israel, meanwhile, has detected, tracked, and in some cases launched strikes against IRGC targets and Iranian supply routes to Hezbollah. While the United Nations theoretically was to prevent Hezbollah's illegal re-armament in the aftermath of the 2006 conflict, today Hezbollah has more artillery and long-range missiles than it had in its possession a decade ago. The recent Iranian shopping spree in both Russia and China may augment both the IRGC and Hezbollah capability to strike more accurately with a broader range. In addition, Iran has openly deployed its indigenous UAV technology into Syria and perhaps Lebanon as well. Iranian UAVs fly over Syria's largest city in Aleppo,[9] and so could just as easily fly over the Golan Heights, the Galilee, or into international air paths over Tel Aviv's Ben Gurion International Airport or Israel's smaller regional airports. That Iranian sources openly brag about their development of both ''suicide' drones and new satellite-guided drone navigation capabilities augments concern.[10] Neither Iran nor its proxies need to be able to strike an aircraft or an airport to be successful. Simply interfering with civilian air traffic will likely augment Israel's isolation as airlines suspend service into Tel Aviv.

Nor is the UAV threat the only one looming for Israel. With the discovery of gas fields in the Eastern Mediterranean, Lebanese authorities have asserted a claim to 300 square miles of Israeli waters. Therefore, even though the United Nations formally certified Israel's withdrawal from Lebanon complete, the dispute over the Shebaa Farms/Har Dov notwithstanding, Lebanon has resurrected a new claim that provides Hezbollah nationalist cover to pursue its rearmament and terrorism. Indeed, Hezbollah has bragged that it has been training operatives in underwater

---

[9] "Aghaz 'Amaliyat-e Pehpad-e Iran dar Jonub Halab" ("The Beginning of UAV Operations in South of Aleppo,") *Raja News*, March 1, 2016

[10] Iran Chaharmen 'Azu Bashgah Sazandgan 'Pehpad Masaleh' ba Hadayat Ma Havareha-ye dar Jahan Shod" ("Iran is the Fourth Member of the Satellite-Guided 'Armed UAV' Club.") *Mashegh*, April 1 2016; "'Amaliyat-e Mowafeq Pehpadha-ye Enthari Sepha " ("Successful Operation of Suicide UAV Corps ")," Fars News Agency, February 23, 2013.

sabotage. This not only suggests a new terror capability that it could utilize against Israel, but a direct threat to the many American engineers and oil workers involved in the region.

Conclusion

It is possible to change Iranian behavior. Khomeini released U.S. hostages in 1981 not because of the persistence of diplomacy, but rather because the Iraqi invasion of Iran had made the cost of the Islamic Republic's isolation too great to bear. Then, in 1982, having repelled the bulk of Iraqi forces from Iranian territory, Ayatollah Khomeini briefly considered ending the Iran-Iraq War. The IRGC interceded, and urged no ceasefire until it had achieved its aims not to oust Saddam Hussein but rather to "liberate Jerusalem." There followed six more years of war that claimed the lives of another half million people. Finally, Khomeini got on the radio and likened accepting a ceasefire to drinking from "a chalice of poison." "Taking this decision was more deadly than taking poison. I submitted myself to God's will and drank this drink for his satisfaction," Khomeini declared.[11]

When Iranian leaders are forced, figuratively, to drink from that chalice of poison, they are willing to renounce terrorism and seek peace. Alas, rather than face recession due to its ideological and military aggression, Iran today has at its disposal a hard currency windfall which will enable it to support proxies to pursue its ideological goals with an ease that it has not enjoyed in decades.

Against this backdrop of Iranian empowerment, it is important that the United States recognize that responding to Iranian bluster and complaints with incentive and greater access to the U.S. and European investment and financial markets is counterproductive to regional security. It is also essential to recognize the depth of IRGC involvement in almost every sector to which U.S. and European firms might consider investing. To bolster both U.S. security and that of Israel and other American regional allies requires draining rather than augmenting IRGC coffers. This will ultimately mean not only greater vigilance absent diplomatic subjectivity to IRGC commercial involvement and terror finance, but a concerted military effort to stymie IRGC smuggling across the Persian Gulf and a broader effort to counter both UAVs and submersible threats not only in Iran's littoral waters, but also in the Gulf of Aden, Red Sea, and Eastern Mediterranean.

The U.S. Navy especially should consider its posture into the next decade. The Eastern Mediterranean was just a few years ago a region to sail through or perhaps in which to enjoy a port call. With the increasing reach and capabilities of Iran in and around the Eastern Mediterranean, greater energy interests in its waters, as well as the presence of Islamic State cells in the Sinai Peninsula, Hamas in the Gaza Strip, Russian President Vladimir Putin's announcement of the deployment of a 16-ship Russian task force, and an increasingly erratic Turkey, it is essential that the United States consider whether the Eastern Mediterranean is, in effect, becoming a new Persian

---

[11] Robert Pear. "Khomeini Accepts 'Poison' of Ending the War with Iraq." *New York Times*, July 21, 1988.

Gulf. If so, a comparison between the U.S. force posture in the Persian Gulf versus the U.S. presence in the Eastern Mediterranean can be shocking. In essence, the only U.S. Navy facility in the region is Souda Bay, Crete, hardly sufficient to address myriad threats now impacting the region.

Thank you.

———

Mr. POE. Thank you, Dr. Rubin.

Mr. Schanzer.

STATEMENT OF JONATHAN SCHANZER, PH.D., VICE PRESIDENT FOR RESEARCH, FOUNDATION FOR DEFENSE OF DEMOCRACIES

Mr. SCHANZER. Mr. Chairman, Madam Chairman, on behalf of the Foundation for Defense of Democracies, thank you for inviting me to testify.

I was asked today to talk about the boycott, divestment, and sanctions movement, also known as BDS. This campaign claims to pursue justice for the Palestinians. In truth, many of these groups seek to wage an economic war against Israel.

Members of the committee, I worked as a terrorism finance analyst at the U.S. Treasury from 2004 to 2007. My job was to help freeze the assets of terrorist financiers.

I am out of government now but I continue to monitor trends in the field. FDD recently completed research that tracked employees from organizations implicated by the Federal Government for terrorism finance.

Our research yielded a troubling outcome in the case of three U.S.-based organizations involving the financing of Hamas—a designated terrorist group with a grisly track record of suicide bombings and firing rockets at civilian populations and whose charter openly calls for the annihilation of Israel.

The three now-defunct organizations are Holy Land Foundation for Relief and Development, Kind Hearts for Charitable Humanitarian Development, and the Islamic Association for Palestine.

As it turns out, many individuals who previously worked for or on behalf of these groups now work or fundraise for an Illinois-based organization called American Muslims for Palestine, otherwise known as AMP.

AMP is arguably the leading BDS organization in the U.S. It is a key sponsor of the anti-Israel campus network known as Students for Justice in Palestine, or SJP.

AMP provides money, speakers, training, printed materials and so-called apartheid walls to SJP activists. AMP even has a campus coordinator who orchestrates the BDS activities of SJP and other campus groups nationwide.

The overlap between AMP, Holy Land, Kind Hearts and the Islamic Association for Palestine is striking. For example, Salah Sarsour, a former fundraiser for the Holy Land Foundation, is now an AMP board member and he has twice served as AMP's national conference chairman.

There is also Jamal Said, who is director of the Mosque Foundation, which prosecutors identified as the key funder for the Holy Land Foundation. And as a reminder, a Federal court found that Holy Land sent $12 million to Hamas over 10 years.

Today, the Mosque Foundation donates to AMP, and Mr. Said has been a keynote speaker at AMP's annual fundraising dinner for 3 years running.

Then there is Abdelbasset Hamayel, who is officially the registered agent for AMP. He is occasionally identified as AMP's director. Several sources point to Hamayel as the Wisconsin and Illinois representative for Kind Hearts, a group the Treasury called the progeny of the Holy Land Foundation. Treasury blocked the assets of Kind Hearts and it was ultimately dissolved.

Hamayel, I should note, was also the secretary general of the Islamic Association for Palestinian, or IAP, a group found civilly liable in a Federal court for financing Hamas, and there are many other IAP-AMP connections.

For example, the former president of IAP, Rafeeq Jaber, is one prominent AMP figure. He has also been listed as the tax preparer for AMP's 501(c)(3) fiscal sponsor since 2010. I am referring here to Americans for Justice in Palestine educational foundation, also known as AJP.

There is also Osama Abuirshaid, who ran IAP's newspaper. He is currently the national coordinator and policy director for AMP. Mr. Abuirshaid also runs a pro-Hamas newspaper in Virginia.

Incidentally, we discovered that a major donor to AMP's conferences, the Zakat Foundation, is run by Khalil Demir. Demir signed the IRS 990 form for Benevolence International Foundation, which Treasury shut down for funding al-Qaeda.

There is also an unregistered BDS group that works with AMP whose leader was reportedly a fighter for the popular front for the liberation of Palestine, also a designated terrorist group.

There is more and so please read my testimony for the full picture. I should note here that our open source research did not indicate that AMP or any of these individuals are currently involved in illegal activity.

But I should also note that AMP, at their 2014 annual conference, held a panel inviting guests to ''come navigate the fine line between legal activism and material support for terrorism.''

It is also noteworthy that a recent photo from AMP suburban Chicago headquarters features a poster with the phrase, ''No Jew will live among them in Jerusalem.''

This sounds a lot like promoting Hamas' agenda here in the United States, if you ask me.

In short, the BDS campaign may pose a threat to Israel but the network I describe here is decidedly an American problem.

There appear to be flaws in the Federal and state oversight of nonprofit and charities. In my written testimony, I suggest ways to increase transparency.

Let me conclude with this. BDS activists are free to say what they want, whether true or false. But tax-advantaged organizations are obliged to be transparent. Americans have a right to know who is leading the BDS campaign and so do the students who may not be aware of AMP's leaders or their goals.

One again, thank you for inviting me to testify and I look forward to your questions.

[The prepared statement of Mr. Schanzer follows:]

Israel Imperiled: Threats to the Jewish State

Jonathan Schanzer
Vice President of Research
Foundation for Defense of Democracies

Joint Hearing before House Foreign Affairs Committee
Subcommittee on Terrorism, Nonproliferation, and Trade and
the Subcommittee on the Middle East and North Africa

Washington, DC
April 19, 2016

DEFENSE OF DEMOCRACIES

1800 M Street NW • Suite 800, South Tower • Washington, DC 20036

Foundation for Defense of Democracies   www.defenddemocracy.org

Chairman Poe, Chairman Ros-Lehtinen, Ranking Member Keating, Ranking Member Deutch, and distinguished members of this subcommittee, on behalf of the Foundation for Defense of Democracies, thank you for the opportunity to testify today.

I was asked to focus my written testimony today on a relatively new, non-kinetic, and less-understood threat to Israel: the Boycott, Divestment, and Sanctions (BDS) campaign. The campaign's goal is to wage an economic and cultural war against the State of Israel. As one of the campaign's founders said, "Palestinians can develop their 'Qassams' [rockets] forever, but that will never hurt Israel as much as a sustained boycott campaign."[1] While these activists are far from achieving their goal, they continue to mount a campaign designed to discourage business with Israel and to delegitimize it. Their ranks appear to be growing – both on college campuses and in communities across the country.[2] Much has been written about this issue, but there has been little scrutiny of the corporate and fiscal structure of the BDS campaign's major actors in the United States. I will focus my remarks on one of those major actors today.

Context

Mr. Chairman, Madam Chairman, I had the honor of working as a terrorism finance analyst for the United States Department of the Treasury from 2004 and 2007. I witnessed firsthand how Treasury has driven many of the world's terrorist financiers out of the country. However, after notching eight terrorist designations of domestic charities over the last 15 years,[3] the pace has slowed to a crawl. It is unclear whether the U.S. government even monitors the activities of individuals who previously worked for charities that were designated or were otherwise found liable for terrorist financing activity.

Members of the Committee, FDD recently conducted research that endeavored to track the activities of former employees from organizations targeted by the U.S government for terrorism finance violations. Our research yielded a surprising and troubling outcome. In the case of three organizations that were designated, shut down, or held civilly liable for providing material support to the terrorist organization Hamas, a significant contingent of their former leadership appears to have pivoted to leadership positions within the American BDS campaign.

The Holy Land Foundation for Relief and Development (HLF), the Islamic Association for Palestine (IAP), and KindHearts for Charitable Development were three organizations implicated in financing Hamas between 2001 and 2011. While members of the organizations' leadership were jailed, deported, or otherwise brought to justice, many high-level and mid-level figures

---

[1] Silvia Cattori, "Omar Barghouti: 'No State Has the Right to Exist as a Racist State,'" *Voltairenet.org*, December 7, 2007. (http://www.voltairenet.org/article153536.html)

[2] Tia Goldenberg, "Growing BDS Movement Raises Alarm Among Israeli Leaders," *Haaretz* (Israel), July 7, 2015. (http://www.haaretz.com/middle-east-news/1.664833)

[3] Holy Land Foundation (2001), Benevolence International Foundation (2002), Global Relief Foundation (2002), Islamic American Relief Agency (2004), Al-Haramain Islamic Foundation (2004), Goodwill Charitable Organization (2007), Tamil Rehabilitation Organization (2007), and Tamil Foundation (2009).
U.S. Department of the Treasury, "Designated Charities and Potential Fundraising Front Organizations for FTOs (listed by affiliation and designation date)," April 5, 2016. (https://www.treasury.gov/resource-center/terrorist-illicit-finance/Pages/protecting-fto.aspx)

remained in the United States. This testimony will show that many of them have gravitated to a new organization called American Muslims for Palestine (AMP).

AMP is a Chicago-based organization that is a leading driver of the BDS campaign. AMP is arguably the most important sponsor and organizer for Students for Justice in Palestine (SJP), which is the most visible arm of the BDS campaign on campuses in the United States. AMP provides speakers, training, printed materials, a so-called "Apartheid Wall," and grants to SJP activists.[4] AMP even has a campus coordinator on staff whose job is to work directly with SJP and other pro-BDS campus groups across the country.[5] According to an email it sent to subscribers, AMP spent $100,000 on campus activities in 2014 alone.[6]

AMP partners with a wide range of BDS organizations,[7] and openly calls for Congress to embrace BDS.[8] According to available records, AMP is a not-for-profit corporation, but not a federal,[9] 501c3, tax-exempt organization.[10] Therefore, AMP does not have to file an IRS 990 form that would make its finances more transparent. AMP instead receives tax-exempt donations through its fiscal sponsor, the Americans for Justice in Palestine Educational Foundation (AJP), which is a 501c3.[11] AMP and AJP are co-located and share officers,[12] yet they remain legally distinct entities after years of nominal separation.

The corporate structure of AMP is cause for concern, but it pales in comparison to the significant overlap between AMP and people who worked for or on behalf of organizations that were designated, dissolved, or held civilly liable by federal authorities for supporting Hamas.

---

[4] Kristin Szremski, "Campus Activism Resources," *American Muslims for Palestine*, September 8, 2014. (http://www.ampalestine.org/index.php/component/content/article/9-projects-a-events/595-campus-activism-resources); "Campus Activism Track," *American Muslims for Palestine*, December 1, 2014, accessed via the Wayback Machine.
(https://web.archive.org/web/20141201172244/http://conference.ampalestine.org/index.php/component/content/article/2-uncategorised/65-campus-activism-track)

[5] "AMP Staff," *American Muslims for Palestine*, accessed April 15, 2016.
(http://www.ampalestine.org/index.php/about-amp/amp-staff)

[6] Email to Subscribers, "Help us make Palestine a household word," *American Muslims for Palestine*, December 30, 2014.

[7] Press Release, "Coalition demands Airbnb remove vacation listings from Israeli settlements." *American Muslims for Palestine*, March 7, 2016. (http://www.ampalestine.org/index.php/newsroom/press-releases/682-coalition-demands-airbnb-remove-vacation-listings-from-israeli-settlements-in-occupied-west-bank); "Member Organizations," *U.S. Campaign to End the Israeli Occupation*, accessed April 15, 2016.
(http://www.endtheoccupation.org/groups.php)

[8] "Tell Congress to hold BDS hearing," *American Muslims for Palestine*, July 30, 2015.
(http://www.ampalestine.org/index.php/take-action/action-alerts/661-tell-congress-to-hold-bds-hearing)

[9] Illinois Secretary of State Business Services, Corporate Filing, "American Muslims for Palestine Inc.," File Number 66688003, accessed April 15, 2016. (http://www.ilsos.gov/corporatellc/CorporateLlcController)

[10] Internal Revenue Service, "Exemption Requirements - 501(c)(3) Organizations," accessed April 15, 2016. (https://www.irs.gov/Charities-&-Non-Profits/Charitable-Organizations/Exemption-Requirements-Section-501(c)(3)-Organizations)

[11] "Are donations to AMP tax exempt?" *American Muslims for Palestine*, accessed April 15, 2016. (http://www.ampalestine.org/index.php/about-amp/amp-faq/219-are-donations-to-amp-tax-exempt)

[12] Internal Revenue Service, *Form 990: Return of Organization Exempt from Income Tax*, "AJP Educational Foundation Inc.," 2014, accessed via GuideStar. (http://www.guidestar.org/FinDocuments//2014/271/365/2014-271365284-0ba3397f-9.pdf)

The Holy Land Foundation

The U.S. Treasury's December 2001 designation of the Richardson, Texas-based Holy Land Foundation was a landmark terrorism finance case in America.[13] As the accompanying Treasury announcement noted, Khaled Meshal, the leader of Hamas, identified HLF officer Mohammed El-Mezain as Hamas's leader in the United States.[14] From 1995 to 2001, according to U.S. government estimates, "HLF sent approximately $12.4 million outside of the United States with the intent to willfully contribute funds, goods, and services to Hamas."[15] In total, seven officials of the Holy Land Foundation were indicted; two of them fled the country and five were eventually sent to prison for providing material support to Hamas.[16]

As it turns out, three individuals from HLF now work for or on behalf of American Muslims for Palestine:

According to its website, Hossein Khatib is a board member for AMP.[17] He was previously a Holy Land Foundation regional director.[18]

Jamal Said, who was the 2014, 2015, and 2016 keynote speaker at AMP fundraisers,[19] raised money for HLF as the director of the Mosque Foundation, a 501c3 organization that donated money to the HLF.[20] Said is still the director of the Mosque Foundation, which is a sponsor of AMP.[21] Said was never charged with any crime, but rather was named by the prosecutors as an unindicted co-conspirator in the Holy Land Foundation trial.[22]

---

[13] U.S. Department of the Treasury, "Protecting Charitable Organizations - E." accessed April 15, 2016. (http://www.treasury.gov/resource-center/terrorist-illicit-finance/Pages/protecting-charities_execorder_13224-e.aspx)

[14] U.S. Department of the Treasury, Press Release, "Treasury Freezes Assets of Organization Tied to Hamas," February 19, 2006. (http://www.treasury.gov/press-center/press-releases/Pages/js4058.aspx)

[15] *United States of America v. Mohammad El-Mezain, et al.*, Appeal, 09-10560 (Court of Appeals Fifth Circuit, December 7, 2011), page 9. (http://www.ca5.uscourts.gov/opinions%5Cpub%5C09/09-10560-CR0.wpd.pdf)

[16] U.S. Department of Justice, Press Release, "Federal Judge Hands Downs Sentences in Holy Land Foundation Case," May 27, 2009. (http://www.justice.gov/opa/pr/federal-judge-hands-downs-sentences-holy-land-foundation-case)

[17] "AMP National Board," *American Muslims for Palestine*, accessed April 15, 2016. (http://www.ampalestine.org/index.php/about-amp/amp-national-board)

[18] "Hussein Khatib," *LinkedIn*, accessed January 12, 2015. (https://www.linkedin.com/profile/view?id=100176222&authType=NAME_SEARCH&authToken=6PVm&locale=en_US&srchid=3641870051421096965128&srchindex=4&srchtotal=20&trk=vsrp_people_res_name&trkInfo=VSRPsearchId%3A3641870051421096965128%2CVSRPtargetId%3A100176222%2CVSRPcmpt%3Aprimary)

[19] AMP-Chicago, "AMP Annual Fundraising Dinner," *Facebook*, March 19, 2014. (https://www.facebook.com/ampalestinechicago/photos/gm.1407041112890451/597477577008212/?type=3&theater); AMP-Chicago. "AMP Fundraising Dinner." *Facebook*. April 18, 2015. (https://www.facebook.com/events/1568230430114028/); AMP-Chicago, "AMP Fundraising Dinner," *Facebook*, March 5, 2016. (https://www.facebook.com/events/1693121294239623/)

[20] Joel Mowbray, "Reign of the Radicals," *The Wall Street Journal*, January 27, 2006. (http://www.wsj.com/articles/SB113832728441457779)

[21] Conference Program, "Thank You To Our Sponsors," *American Muslims for Palestine*, 2015, page 6.

[22] Andrea Elliott, "White House Quietly Courts Muslims in US," *The New York Times*, April 18, 2010. (http://www.nytimes.com/2010/04/19/us/politics/19muslim.html)

Salah Sarsour is an AMP board member.[23] A 2001 FBI memo to the U.S. Treasury's Office of Foreign Assets Control (OFAC) describes how Sarsour's brother, after being arrested by Israel in 1998, told Israeli officials about Sarsour's "involvement with Hamas and fundraising activities of HLFRD [Holy Land Foundation for Relief and Development]."[24]

At AMP's 2015 conference, Sarsour was identified as the conference chairman.[25] On the advertising and sponsorship page for the conference, non-profits that wish to donate to or advertise with AMP are instructed to contact Sarsour.[26] Sarsour told *Al-Jazeera* "that the conference aims to keep up with and support the Palestinian people's continuous intifada."[27]

Sarsour's past is cause for concern. According to Israeli sources cited in a book by former FBI and U.S. Treasury official Matthew Levitt, Sarsour's brother, Jamil Sarsour, told Israeli authorities that he and Salah used their Milwaukee furniture store's bank account to pass money to Adel Awadallah,[28] who was then a leader of the Qassam Brigades, Hamas's armed wing.[29] According to Jamil, Salah Sarsour and Awadallah had become friends while sharing a prison cell.[30] Salah Sarsour spent eight months in jail in Israel for his Hamas activity.[31]

By way of background, Hamas politburo figure Mousa Abu Marzook gave HLF $210,000 in startup funds.[32] According to the U.S. Department of the Treasury, Marzook tapped "HLF as the

[23] "AMP National Board," *American Muslims for Palestine*, accessed April 15, 2016. (http://www.ampalestine.org/index.php/about-amp/amp-national-board)
[24] FBI Memo to the U.S. Department of the Treasury, "Holy Land Foundation For Relief And Development International Emergency Economic Powers Act," November 1, 2001. (http://www.copleydc.net/cns_links/terrorism/fbi%20report.pdf)
[25] Email to Subscribers, "A letter from AMP Conference Chairman Salah Sarsour," *American Muslims for Palestine*, December 1, 2014.
[26] "Sponsor the Conference," *American Muslims for Palestine*, accessed April 15, 2016. (http://conference.ampalestine.org/index.php/sponsorship)
[27] Abdul Jaleel Al-Bukhari, "مؤتمر فلسطين بأميركا يسائل الحاضر والمستقبل" (Palestine Conference in the United States Explores the Present and the Future)," *Al Jazeera* (Qatar), November 30, 2015. (http://www.aljazeera.net/news/reportsandinterviews/2015/11/30/مؤتمر-فلسطين-بأميركا-يسائل-الحاضر-والمستقبل)
[28] Matthew Levitt, *Hamas: Politics, Charity, and Terrorism in the Service of Jihad*, (New Haven, CT: Yale University Press, 2006), page 78.
[29] Barbara Demick, "Israeli Security Force Kills Two Top Hamas Terrorists," *The Philadelphia Inquirer*, September 12, 1998. (http://articles.philly.com/1998-09-12/news/25757281_1_imad-awadallah-adel-awadallah-dozens-of-israeli-army)
[30] Matthew Levitt, *Hamas: Politics, Charity, and Terrorism in the Service of Jihad*, (New Haven, CT: Yale University Press, 2006), page 78. See also: Laurie Cohen and Kim Barker, "Target of Hamas fundraising probe here charged in Wisconsin," *Chicago Tribune*, January 07, 2003. (http://articles.chicagotribune.com/2003-01-07/news/0301070192_1_hamas-activist-federal-charges-israeli)
[31] "Profile: American Muslims for Palestine," *Anti-Defamation League*, 2013. (http://www.adl.org/assets/pdf/israel-international/american-muslims-for-palestine-2013-03-29-v1.pdf)
[32] Eric Lichtblau and Judith Miller, "Threats and Responses: The Money Trail; 5 Brothers Charged With Aiding Hamas," *The New York Times*, December 19, 2002. (http://www.nytimes.com/2002/12/19/us/threats-and-responses-the-money-trail-5-brothers-charged-with-aiding-hamas.html)

primary fund-raising entity for HAMAS [sic] in the United States."[33] The U.S. Treasury designated Marzook as a terrorist in 1995, and deported him in 1997.[34]

The Islamic Association for Palestine

The Islamic Association for Palestine (IAP) is another organization that raised money and provided material support for Hamas in America. Like HLF, IAP was founded with money from Abu Marzook.[35] In 2004, the organization was found civilly liable in a federal district court for supporting Hamas.[36] The defendants appealed, but a federal appeals court upheld the judgment in 2008.[37] IAP disbanded in 2010.[38] According to evidence presented at the HLF trial, "numerous donation checks ... made payable to ... IAP" were "deposited into HLF's bank account," in some cases with the memo line, "for Palestinian Mujahideen [holy warriors] only."[39]

FDD research again found significant overlap between employees from this Hamas-supporting organization and the American Muslims for Palestine network.

Rafeeq Jaber is the former president of IAP.[40] AMP's tax-exempt arm, the AJP Educational Foundation, listed him as its tax preparer in their most recent public filing.[41] Jaber's official role with AMP is unclear: he appears on their 2010 through 2014 IRS forms as their tax preparer,[42] but he does not appear on AMP's website. He has been identified in the Palestinian press as the "spiritual father" of AMP's coalitions with other Muslim-American organizations,[43] and he

[33] U.S. Department of the Treasury, "Protecting Charitable Organizations - E," accessed August 21, 2007. (http://www.treasury.gov/resource-center/terrorist-illicit-finance/Pages/protecting-charities_execorder_13224-c.aspx)
[34] "Hamas out of Syria, Marzook says," *Associated Press*, February 27, 2012. (http://www.ynetnews.com/articles/0,7340,L-4195457,00.html)
[35] *United States District Court Northern District of Texas, USA v. Holy Land Foundation for Relief and Development*, "Payments from Marzook to the Islamic Association for Palestine," (Northern District of Texas, September 29, 2008), accessed April 15, 2016. (http://coop.txnd.uscourts.gov/judges/hlf2/09-29-08/Marzook%20IAP.pdf)
[36] Laurie Cohen, "3 Islamic fundraisers held liable in terror death," *Chicago Tribune*, November 11, 2004. (http://articles.chicagotribune.com/2004-11-11/news/0411110231_1_david-boim-magistrate-judge-arlander-keys-joyce-boim)
[37] "Anti-Terrorism Judgment Upheld Against U.S. Charities," *Anti-Defamation League*, December 18 2008. (http://archive.adl.org/main_terrorism/boim_upheld.html#.VLg28v5RLGA)
[38] Texas Secretary of State, Corporate Filing, "Islamic Association for Palestine," Tax ID 30116732022, accessed April 15, 2016. (https://mycpa.cpa.state.tx.us/coa/servlet/cpa.app.coa.CoaGetTp)
[39] *United States of America v. Mohammad El-Mezain, et al.*, Appeal, 09-10560 (Court of Appeals Fifth Circuit, December 7, 2011). page 170. (http://www.ca5.uscourts.gov/opinions%5Cpub%5C09/09-10560-CR0.wpd.pdf)
[40] "IAP Contact Information," *Islamic Association for Palestine*, April 7, 2003, accessed via Wayback Machine. (http://web.archive.org/web/20030407164156/http://www.iap.org/contactus.htm)
[41] Internal Revenue Service, *Form 990: Return of Organization Exempt from Income Tax*, "AJP Educational Foundation Inc.," 2014, accessed via GuideStar. (http://www.guidestar.org/FinDocuments//2014/271/365/2014-271365284-0ba3397f-9.pdf)
[42] For the most recent, see: Internal Revenue Service, *Form 990: Return of Organization Exempt from Income Tax*, "AJP Educational Foundation Inc.," 2014, accessed via GuideStar. (http://www.guidestar.org/FinDocuments//2014/271/365/2014-271365284-0ba3397f-9.pdf)
[43] "مئات الآلاف في شوارع المدن الأمريكية نصرة لغزة" (Hundreds of Thousands in the Streets of American Cities in Support of Gaza)," *Ma'an News Agency* (Palestinian Territories), August 11, 2014. (http://maannews.net/Content.aspx?id=719809)

signed a September 2015 petition as a representative of AMP.[44] His financial services business is currently listed at the same office building where IAP was located before it was shut down.[45]

There is also Abdelbasset Hamayel, who served as IAP's secretary general.[46] Today, he is AMP's registered agent in Chicago.[47] Interestingly, he is not listed as an officer or executive on AMP's tax forms or website. His name, however, appears on the AJP Educational Foundation's IRS 990 form as the person "who possesses the organization's books and records."[48] Hamayel signed a September 2015 petition as the "Director of American Muslims for Palestine, Chicago."[49] Similarly, one AMP Facebook post labels Hamayel as the group's "Executive Director."[50]

Sufian Nabhan is another AMP board member.[51] He was IAP's former Michigan representative.[52]

Osama Abuirshaid is identified by AMP as its "National Coordinator"[53] or "National Policy Director."[54] In August 2015, the United States Citizenship and Immigration Services issued an initial determination that Abuirshaid was "ineligible for naturalization" because he failed to properly disclose his IAP past.[55] Abuirshaid was the editor of IAP's newspaper, *Al Zaytounah*.[56] Today, he runs a newspaper called *Al-Meezan* that includes articles praising Hamas.[57]

---

[44] "Petition to ISNA Leadership to do more for Syria," *Change.org*, September 3, 2015.
(https://www.change.org/p/isna-leadership-president-secretary-gen-and-majlis-ash-shura-petition-to-isna-leadership-to-do-more-for-syria)

[45] "Jaber Financial Services," *Cortera*, accessed April 15, 2016.
(http://start.cortera.com/company/research/k5m5qyr4s/jaber-financial-services-inc/); "IAP Contact Information," *Islamic Association for Palestine*, April 7, 2003, accessed via Wayback Machine.
(http://web.archive.org/web/20030407164156/http://www.iap.org/contactus.htm)

[46] "IAP Contact Information," *Islamic Association for Palestine*, April 7, 2003, accessed via Wayback Machine.
(http://web.archive.org/web/20030407164156/http://www.iap.org/contactus.htm)

[47] Illinois Secretary of State Business Services, Corporate Filing, "American Muslims for Palestine Inc.," File Number 66688003, accessed April 10, 2016. (http://www.ilsos.gov/corporatellc/CorporateLlcController)

[48] Internal Revenue Service, *Form 990: Return of Organization Exempt from Income Tax*, "AJP Educational Foundation Inc.," 2014, accessed via GuideStar. (http://www.guidestar.org/FinDocuments//2014/271/365/2014-271365284-0ba3397f-9.pdf)

[49] "Petition to ISNA Leadership to do more for Syria," *Change.org*, September 3, 2015.
(https://www.change.org/p/isna-leadership-president-secretary-gen-and-majlis-ash-shura-petition-to-isna-leadership-to-do-more-for-syria)

[50] AMP-Chicago, *Facebook*, August 29, 2014.
(https://www.facebook.com/ampalestinechicago/photos/pb.550789245010379.-2207520000.1459717920./681386211950681/?type=3&theater)

[51] "AMP National Board," *American Muslims for Palestine*, accessed April 15, 2016.
(http://www.ampalestine.org/index.php/about-amp/amp-national-board)

[52] "IAP Contact Information," *Islamic Association for Palestine*, April 7, 2003, accessed via Wayback Machine.
(http://web.archive.org/web/20030407164156/http://www.iap.org/contactus.htm)

[53] Press Release, "Latest bus ad causes stir in DC," *American Muslims for Palestine*, February 24, 2015.
(http://www.ampalestine.org/index.php/newsroom/press-releases/627-new-bus-ad-takes-on-israel-us-relationship-on-eve-of-netanyahu-s-address-to-congress)

[54] Press Release, "AMP condemns attack on Al Aqsa; youth," *American Muslims for Palestine*, September 16, 2015.
(http://www.ampalestine.org/index.php/newsroom/statements/666-amp-condemns-attack-on-al-aqsa-youth)

[55] *Abuirshaid v. Johnson et al*, No. 1:2015cv01113 (Virginia Eastern District Court, August 31, 2015).
(https://dockets.justia.com/docket/virginia/vaedce/1:2015cv01113/327963)

KindHearts

Before it was shut down, IAP raised money for another organization called KindHearts for Charitable Development.[58] Founded in 2002, KindHearts was based in Toledo, Ohio. In 2006, the Treasury Department used a mechanism known as a Block Pending Investigation (BPI) to freeze the assets of KindHearts, stating that the organization was the "progeny" of HLF, and that it provided "support for terrorism behind the façade of charitable giving."[59] In 2011, after a lengthy battle with the U.S. government over the legality of the BPI, KindHearts agreed to disband and its assets were redistributed to other organizations.[60]

Legal challenges notwithstanding, Treasury stated that "KindHearts officials and fundraisers have coordinated with Hamas leaders and made contributions to Hamas-affiliated organizations." Treasury further asserted that "KindHearts deposited the funds into the same account used by HLF when it was providing funds" overseas.[61] KindHearts also paid IAP more than $77,000 to do its fundraising and other activities, according to the group's 2003 IRS 990 forms.[62]

KindHearts's president was Khaled Smaili, a former official of the Global Relief Foundation (GRF).[63] GRF was officially registered as a charity in Palos Hills, Illinois. In 2002, Treasury designated GRF as a "Specially Designated Global Terrorist" for funding al-Qaeda.[64]

Several sources point to former IAP Secretary General Abdelbasset Hamayel as having also served as KindHearts' Illinois representative.[65] For example, one graphic design firm posted

[56] "Profile: American Muslims for Palestine," *Anti-Defamation League*, 2003. (http://www.adl.org/assets/pdf/israel-international/american-muslims-for-palestine-2013-03-29-v1.pdf)

[57] كتائب القسام.. من بندقية متواضعة إلى جيش عسكري منظم (Qassam Brigades: From Humble Rifle to Organized Army)." *Al-Meezan News*, May 1, 2015, page 10. (http://almeezannews.com/PDFs/almeezanPDF_248.pdf); " مدونة للأستاذ شكري أبو بكر على الإنترنت (Mr. Shukri's Bakr's Blog on the Internet)." *Al-Meezan News*, May 1, 2015, page 2. (http://www.almeezannews.com/PDFs/almeezanPDF_268.pdf)

[58] Internal Revenue Service, *Form 990: Return of Organization Exempt from Income Tax*, "KindHearts for Charitable Development, Inc.," 2003, accessed via The Foundation Center. (http://990s.foundationcenter.org/990_pdf_archive/020/020534702/020534702_200312_990.pdf?_ga=1.209492948.777103848.1460262044)

[59] U.S. Department of the Treasury, Press Release. "Treasury Freezes Assets of Organization Tied to Hamas," February 19, 2006. (http://www.treasury.gov/press-center/press-releases/Pages/js4058.aspx)

[60] "Settlement Agreement," *American Civil Liberties Union*, November 2011. (https://www.aclu.org/files/assets/KindHearts_v__geithner_-_settlement.pdf)

[61] U.S. Department of the Treasury, Press Release. "Treasury Freezes Assets of Organization Tied to Hamas," February 19, 2006. (http://www.treasury.gov/press-center/press-releases/Pages/js4058.aspx)

[62] Internal Revenue Service, *Form 990: Return of Organization Exempt from Income Tax*, "KindHearts for Charitable Development, Inc.," 2003, accessed via The Foundation Center. (http://990s.foundationcenter.org/990_pdf_archive/020/020534702/020534702_200312_990.pdf?_ga=1.209492948.777103848.1460262044)

[63] U.S. Department of the Treasury, Press Release. "Treasury Freezes Assets of Organization Tied to Hamas," February 19, 2006. (http://www.treasury.gov/press-center/press-releases/Pages/js4058.aspx)

[64] U.S Department of the Treasury, Press Release. "Treasury Department Statement Regarding the Designation of the Global Relief Foundation," October 18, 2002. (https://www.treasury.gov/press-center/press-releases/Pages/po3553.aspx)

[65] Steven Emerson, "Money Laundering and Terror Financing Issues in the Middle East," *Testimony before the Senate Committee on Banking, Housing, and Urban Affairs*, July 13, 2005.

Hamayel's business card on its website, identifying him as KindHeart's "Illinois and Wisconsin Representative."[66] Additionally, a KindHeart's poster for a 2004 fundraiser lists Abaset@Kind-Hearts.org as the point of contact.[67] As noted above, Hamayel is currently listed on AMP's website as the group's registered agent,[68] and he is listed on AJP's 990 forms as the person "who possesses the organization's books and records."[69]

AMP Donors with a Troubled Past

In short, at least seven individuals who work for or on behalf of AMP have worked for or on behalf of organizations previously shut down or held civilly liable in the United States for providing financial support to Hamas: the Holy Land Foundation, the Islamic Association for Palestine, and KindHearts.

AMP states that it was founded in 2005. They were, in their words, "a strictly volunteer organization" until 2008, when they opened their national headquarters in Palos Hills, Illinois.[70] Their mission statement does not include raising money for causes abroad, and we have seen no evidence of illicit activity. Its mission, however, is troubling. A recent photo from their headquarters features an Arabic-language poster that includes the phrase, "No Jew will live among them in Jerusalem."[71] It is also troubling that at their 2014 annual conference, AMP invited participants to "navigate the fine line between legal activism and material support for terrorism."[72] That invitation is troubling because it appears that some of AMP's officers and donors came from organizations that have failed to navigate that "fine line" in the past.

One business that supports AMP is Middle East Financial Services (MEFS). The company has offices in Palos Hills, Illinois and in Dearborn, Michigan, and several affiliates abroad.[73] MEFS

(http://www.banking.senate.gov/public/_cache/files/d2b01fcf-a768-45d3-9d9d-436f93ee5f9e/33A699FF535D59925B69836A6E068FD0.emerson.pdf)

[66] "KindHearts Business Cards with Names," *Sakkal Design Graphic Design and Illustrations*, accessed April 15, 2016. (http://www.sakkal.com/Graphics/logos/kindheart/kindhearts_bc03.html)

[67] Flier, "Annual Fund Raising Dinner for Palestine & KindHearts' Annual Contest," *KindHearts Charitable Humanitarian Development*. April 23, 2005, accessed via WayBack Machine. (http://web.archive.org/web/20050515004402/http://www.kind-hearts.org/upcoming%20event/set%204%20printout.pdf)

[68] Illinois Secretary of State Business Services, Corporate Filing, "American Muslims for Palestine, Inc.," File Number 66688003, accessed April 15, 2016. (http://www.ilsos.gov/corporatellc/CorporateLlcController)

[69] Internal Revenue Service, *Form 990: Return of Organization Exempt from Income Tax*, "AJP Educational Foundation Inc.," 2014, accessed via GuideStar. (http://www.guidestar.org/FinDocuments//2014/271/365/2014-271365284-0ba3397f-9.pdf)

[70] "When was AMP formed?" *American Muslims for Palestine*, accessed April 15, 2016. (http://www.ampalestine.org/index.php/about-amp/amp-faq/214-when-was-amp-formed)

[71] The poster is the text of a document called "Umar's Assurance," issued when the Muslims conquered Jerusalem during the Arab-Byzantine wars in 637 AD. AMP-Chicago, *Facebook*, May 3, 2015. (https://www.facebook.com/ampalestinechicago/photos/pb.550789245010379.-2207520000.1441917522./812588892163745/?type=1&theater)

[72] Shane Harris, "Pro-Palestinian Group Lectured on Skirting Terror Laws," *The Daily Beast*, December 5, 2014. (http://www.thedailybeast.com/articles/2014/12/05/pro-palestinian-group-lectured-on-skirting-terror-laws.html)

[73] "Countries," *Middle East Financial Services*, accessed April 15, 2016. (http://mefs.us/)

was a "bronze sponsor" to the AMP convention in 2014 and advertised at their 2015 conference.[74]

MEFS itself has never been charged with being complicit in terrorism financing, and we have no evidence that it has been, but its services have been used by some who have. MEFS was used in 2002 to wire money to Palestinian Islamic Jihad (PIJ), which the State Department designated as a terrorist group in 1997. Salah Daoud, a former MEFS employee and IAP board member, testified in court in 2005 about how one of IAP's volunteers, Hatem Fariz, used MEFS over several months to send approximately $60,000 to PIJ.[75] Fariz was sentenced to 37 months in a U.S. prison for "conspiracy to make or receive contributions of funds, goods, or services to or for the benefit of a Specially Designated Terrorist."[76] Daoud, who testified in exchange for immunity, was never charged with a crime.[77]

Another interesting supporter of AMP is Prime Furniture Wholesale in Milwaukee.[78] This store is owned by AMP board member Salah Sarsour,[79] who, as noted above, reportedly used the bank account of his family's furniture store in the 1990s to send money to Qassam Brigades commander Adel Awadallah.[80]

Finally, there is the Zakat Foundation. The Foundation's executive director is Khalil Demir.[81] Demir signed the IRS 990 forms[82] for a group Treasury designated in 2002 for funding al-Qaeda: Benevolence International Foundation (BIF).[83] The Zakat Foundation was a "platinum sponsor"

---

[74] Conference Program, *American Muslims for Palestine*, 2014, page 29; Conference Program, *American Muslims for Palestine*. 2015, page 6.
[75] "Witness says Al-Arian co-defendant sent $60,000 to the Middle East," *Associated Press*, June 30, 2005. (http://www.mywebtimes.com/news/illinois_ap/witness-says-al-arian-co-defendant-sent-to-the-middle/article_9533c078-b9c2-522e-9d6e-48fd41be15c3.html); *United States v. Sami Amin Al-Arian et al.*, Transcript of Proceedings, 8:03-CR-77-T-30TBM, (Middle District of Florida Tampa Division, June 29, 2005).
[76] Meg Laughlin, "Al-Arian associate gets prison," *Tampa Bay Times*, July 26, 2006. (http://www.sptimes.com/2006/07/26/Tampabay/Al_Arian_associate_ge.shtml)
[77] "Witness says Al-Arian co-defendant sent $60,000 to the Middle East," *Associated Press*, June 30, 2005. (http://www.mywebtimes.com/news/illinois_ap/witness-says-al-arian-co-defendant-sent-to-the-middle/article_9533c078-b9c2-522e-9d6e-48fd41be15c3.html)
[78] Conference Program, *American Muslims for Palestine*, 2014, page 29; Conference Program, *American Muslims for Palestine*, 2015, page 38.
[79] Wisconsin Department of Financial Institutions, Corporate Filing, "Prime Furniture Wholesale, LLC," accessed April 15, 2016. (https://www.wdfi.org/apps/CorpSearch/Details.aspx?entityID=P057485&hash=1633449285&searchFunctionID=1 2cc3312-59e1-48ad-ad60-4b88c9e6d586&type=Simple&q=prime+furniture+wholesale)
[80] Matthew Levitt, *Hamas: Politics, Charity, and Terrorism in the Service of Jihad*, (New Haven, CT: Yale University Press, 2006), page 78.
[81] "Our Team," *Zakat Foundation of America*, accessed April 15, 2016. (http://www.zakat.org/about/our-team/)
[82] Internal Revenue Service, Form 990: Return of Organization Exempt from Income Tax, "Benevolence International Foundation," 2001, accessed via GuideStar. (http://www.guidestar.org/FinDocuments/2001/363/823/2001-363823186-1-9.pdf). The forms states that "Books are in care of Halil I. Demir."
[83] U.S. Department of the Treasury, Press Release, "Treasury Designates Benevolence International Foundation and Related Entities as Financiers of Terrorism," November 19, 2002. (http://www.treasury.gov/press-center/press-releases/Pages/po3632.aspx)

of AMP's 2014 and 2015 conferences, and was acknowledged for this in the conference programs.[84]

The BDS Campaign in Chicago, the PLO, and the PFLP

Members of the Committee, the network described here prompted our research team to identify other organizations that engage in BDS activity in the Chicago area. We soon discovered an additional organization that does not appear to be registered at the federal or state level.

This group has been alternately described as "The U.S. Coalition to Boycott Israel"[85] and the "Chicago Coalition for Justice in Palestine."[86] The group's president is Chicago resident Ghassan Barakat,[87] a consular notary for the Palestine Liberation Organization (PLO)[88] who has been identified by the Palestinian Expatriates Affairs Department website as a member of the Palestine National Council (PNC).[89] The group's "coordinator" is Senan Shaqdeh.[90] A profile published by the PLO's Expatriates Affairs Department states that Shaqdeh was a "fighter in the ranks of the mountain brigade" for the Popular Front for the Liberation of Palestine,[91] which is a PLO faction that the U.S. designated as a Foreign Terrorist Organization (FTO) in 1997.[92] Shaqdeh also claims to be a founder of Students for Justice in Palestine[93] – the U.S. campus-based network that receives guidance and financial assistance from AMP.

In a PLO YouTube video, Shaqdeh said that he travelled to Ramallah in September 2014 to meet with President Mahmoud Abbas and Prime Minister Rami Hamdallah about BDS activity in

---

[84] Conference Program, *American Muslims for Palestine*, 2014, page 29; Conference Program, *American Muslims for Palestine*, 2015, page 6.

[85] الولايات المتحدة : المجلس الفلسطيني الامريكي يحيي ذكرى يوم الأرض في لوزيانا Palestine Department of Expatriates Affairs, (United States: Palestinian American Council Commemorates Land Day in Louisiana)," April 10, 2015. (http://www.pead.ps/-اخبار-الجاليات/اخبار-الجاليات/جاليات-الولايات-المتحده/1990-الولايات-المتحدة-المجلس-الفلسطيني-الامريكي-يحيي-ذكرى-يوم-الأرض-في-لوزيانا.html)

[86] "Gun toting Zionist arrested at Chicago pro-Israel protest," *FightBack! News*, July 24, 2014. (http://www.fightbacknews.org/2014/7/24/gun-toting-zionist-arrested-chicago-pro-isreal-protest)

[87] الولايات المتحدة : المجلس الفلسطيني الامريكي يحيي ذكرى يوم الأرض في لوزيانا Palestine Department of Expatriates Affairs, (United States: Palestinian American Council Commemorates Land Day in Louisiana)," April 10, 2015. (http://www.pead.ps/-اخبار-الجاليات/اخبار-الجاليات/جاليات-الولايات-المتحده/1990-الولايات-المتحدة-المجلس-الفلسطيني-الامريكي-يحيي-ذكرى-يوم-الأرض-في-لوزيانا.html)

[88] PLO Delegation to the United States, "Designated Notary," accessed April 15, 2016. (https://web.archive.org/web/20150217091605/http://plodelegation.us/consular-affairs/designated-notary/#collapse3)

[89] الولايات المتحدة : المجلس الفلسطيني الامريكي يحيي ذكرى يوم الأرض في لوزيانا Palestine Department of Expatriates Affairs, (United States: Palestinian American Council Commemorates Land Day in Louisiana)," April 10, 2015. (http://www.pead.ps/-اخبار-الجاليات/اخبار-الجاليات/جاليات-الولايات-المتحده/1990-الولايات-المتحدة-المجلس-الفلسطيني-الامريكي-يحيي-ذكرى-يوم-الأرض-في-لوزيانا.html)

[90] "Senan Shaqdeh," *Facebook*, accessed April 15, 2016. (https://www.facebook.com/senans?fref=ts)

[91] Palestine Department of Expatriates Affairs, "سنان شقديح ... بائع البيبسي الذي يقارع إسرائيل (Senan Shaqdeh: The Pepsi Salesman Who is Rebuking Israel)," June 14, 2015. (http://www.pead.ps/-صحافة/صحافة/مقالات-مترجمة/2233-سنان-شقديح-بائع-البيبسي-الذي-يقارع-إسرائيل.html)

[92] U.S. Department of State, "Foreign Terrorist Organizations," accessed April 15, 2016. (http://www.state.gov/j/ct/rls/other/des/123085.htm)

[93] Palestine Department of Expatriates Affairs, "سنان شقديح ... بائع البيبسي الذي يقارع إسرائيل (Senan Shaqdeh: The Pepsi Salesman Who is Rebuking Israel)," June 14, 2015. (http://www.pead.ps/-صحافة/صحافة/مقالات-مترجمة/2233-سنان-شقديح-بائع-البيبسي-الذي-يقارع-إسرائيل.html)

America.[94] Shaqdeh's access to the highest echelons of the Palestinian government, his PFLP past, and his connections to the AMP network may be worthy of further scrutiny.

Recommendations and Conclusion

In conclusion, AMP's BDS campaign may be a headache for Israel, but the fact that it is based in the United States makes it an American issue. The overlap of former employees of organizations that provided support to Hamas who now play important roles in AMP speaks volumes about the real agenda of key components of the BDS campaign.

Mr. Chairman, Madam Chairman, and distinguished members of the committee, there are many aspects of FDD's analysis of this network that I did not address in my testimony. I would be pleased to answer any questions.

In the meantime, I recommend Congress legislate a disclosure process for charity employees and board members previously implicated in terror finance. Unlike some of its European counterparts, the IRS pays scant attention to the prior histories of Section 501 entities and their officers or directors. Nonprofit entities should be required to fully disclose in their IRS form 990 and 1023 the roles of its leadership (board members and executives) in organizations that earned Treasury designations, Treasury actions like Block Pending Investigations (BPI), federal anti-terrorism actions, or litigation in which their organization was found liable for material support for terrorism. These records should be evaluated by the IRS and/or at the state level before nonprofit entities gain initial nonprofit status or continued status as a nonprofit. Failure to disclose this information should result in significant penalties.

I should emphasize here that it is not my place to say where Americans should direct their charitable giving, or what anti-Israel activists may say or do. What I have provided today is simply a network analysis. Americans have a right to know who is behind the BDS campaign. And so do those members of the BDS campaign who may not fully understand its history.

On behalf of the Foundation for Defense of Democracies, thank you again for inviting me to testify.

---

[94] Palestine Department of Expatriates Affairs, " لقاء مع الدكتور سنان شقديح منسق تحالف منظمات مقاطعة اسرائيل في الولايات المتحدة الأمريكية (Meeting with Dr. Sinan Shaqdeh, Coordinator of the Coalition to Boycott Israel in the USA)," *YouTube,* September 2, 2014. (https://www.youtube.com/watch?v=y1fSYvV8cSU)

34

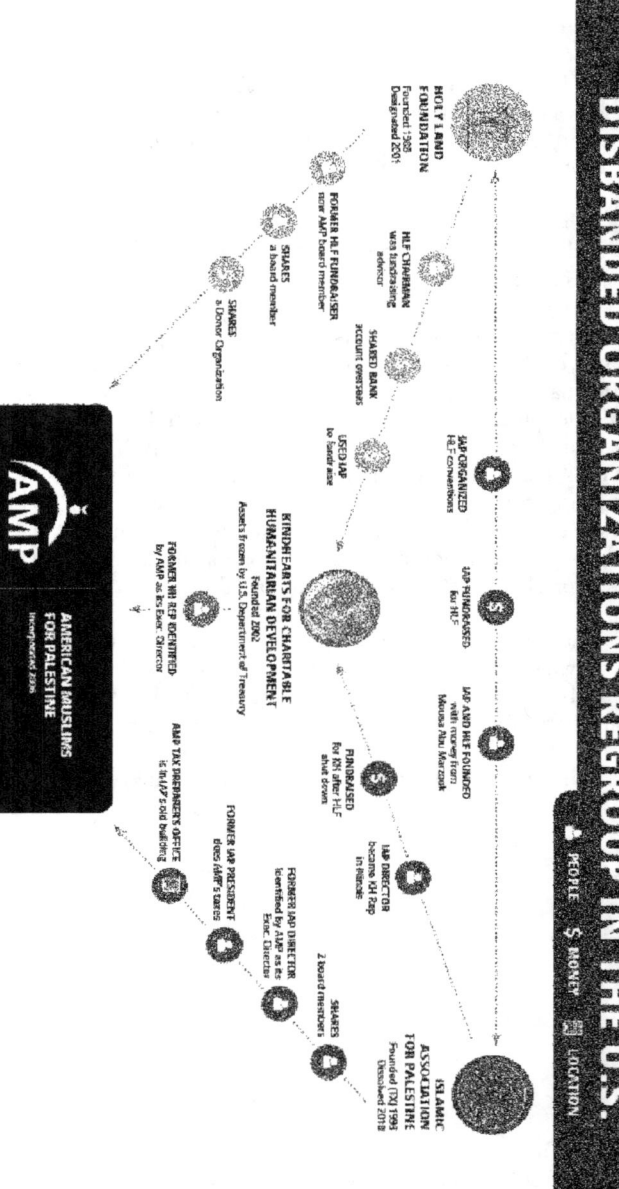

Mr. POE. Mr. Makovsky.

STATEMENT OF MR. DAVID MAKOVSKY, ZIEGLER DISTINGUISHED FELLOW, IRWIN LEVY FAMILY PROGRAM ON THE U.S.-ISRAEL STRATEGIC RELATIONSHIP, THE WASHINGTON INSTITUTE FOR NEAR EAST POLICY

Mr. MAKOVSKY. Mr. Chairman, Madam Chairwoman, ranking members, of course, thank you for the opportunity to speak before these two distinguished subcommittees.

In keeping with the questions you asked us about challenges, I would like to first focus on security in the evolving threat environment.

Israel is largely encircled by nonstate actors today. They have no problem to embed themselves in the heart of urban areas, fire rockets into Israeli cities and in so doing, challenge Israel to retaliate which leads to greater Palestinian casualties.

In Lebanon, the dominant nonstate actor is Hezbollah, which, as you have pointed out, is believed to have 150,000 rockets. Then there is Hamas in Gaza. While there is relative quiet along this front, it's only a matter of time before a fourth war begins in Gaza.

Needless to say, without U.S. military assistance writ large and without Iron Dome specifically, Israel's security predicament would be far worse.

Of course, beyond the challenge of its immediate neighbors there is also Iran and its regional proxies. Israel may not like the Iran deal, as we all know, but understands it must now turn toward enhancing the U.S.-Israel bilateral security relationship, as should the United States as well.

This rather sober assessment has been punctuated by relative success in the Israel-Palestinian security cooperation in the West Bank. Of course, we don't know who did this attack yesterday on the bus. It has the markings of a homemade and not organizational type, which would be consistent. But I would say that Israeli officials say that the PA security cooperation with Israel has been essential in reducing this fact—in reducing the recent wave of violence.

Just last week, Israeli Defense Minister Moshe Ya'alon held a press conference and he said, ''The PA has worked tirelessly recently to stop terror.''

In return, Israel's security services has served as an important stabilizing role within the Israeli structure and promoted further economic and security cooperation with the Palestinians. However, it may still be too soon to pronounce that the wave of stabbing is over, as there could be an upsurge with the upcoming holiday season which begins in the next few days.

So what can the U.S. do to tackle these threats and seize the opportunities? When it comes to Iran, the U.S. and Israel need to strictly enforce Iranian compliance of the nuclear deal and push back against malign Iranian behavior in the region.

The U.S. and Israel should form a joint committee which would deal with the implementation of JCPOA, address the potential violations, and maintain and strengthen nonnuclear sanctions.

The U.S. and Israel should also swiftly conclude negations for a 10-year MOU. Israel's deterrent power, as you know, is in large part a reflection of how its adversaries view the strength of its strategic relationship with Washington.

In a broad sense, Israel views the strength of the U.S.-Israel relationship as a function of how the U.S. is perceived in the region by friend and foe alike.

If the U.S. is viewed as the center of the pragmatic camp in the Middle East, this will bolster the position of this critical bilateral relationship beyond all its other obvious benefits.

On the Palestinian issue, there remain several challenges. The U.S. has engaged in three noble efforts in 2000, 2007, 2014 to solve the entire conflict. For a variety of reasons these efforts didn't succeed.

Under the current leadership, I don't see succeeding in the near future. I'm rather skeptical about efforts to put forward parameters at the U.N. Security Council, which would be interpreted by both sides as an imposed solution and could serve as a baseline for defiance rather than bringing the parties closer.

Indeed, we need to find a way to maintain the viability of a two-state outcome. Even if we can't implement a two-state solution today, I have some ideas which I can discuss when we have more time in the Q and A.

There are also moves the Palestinians could take to prove their commitment to two states as well including jettisoning its anti-normalization policy and stop incentivizing terror by paying money to Palestinian prisoners and relatives of suicide bombers.

U.S. needs to sensitize our European allies to these issue. Given the closeness between the Europeans and the Palestinians, it would carry weight if the Europeans practiced the same tough love they have urged the United States to administer when it comes to Israel. But they don't seem to do it to our Palestinian friends.

The issue of boycott, divestment, and sanctions—BDS—is important to me. I have visited over—made 121 campus visits, mostly to discuss this issue. And if the BDS movement isn't blunted and there is no movement on the ground toward peace, I fear that the movement could metastasize beyond college campuses.

In conclusion, there are definite challenges. But there are also opportunities amid the crises. The dynamism of the U.S.-Israel relationship will be tested by how our two countries work together to meet these new challenges and in so doing take our relationship to the next level.

Thank you very much.

[The prepared statement of Mr. Makovsky follows:]

Testimony before the House Committee on Foreign Affairs
Israel Imperiled: Threats to the Jewish State

David Makovsky
Ziegler Distinguished Fellow and Director, Project on the Middle East Peace Process
The Washington Institute for Near East Policy
April 19th, 2016

Dear Mr. Chairmen and Ranking Members,

Thank you for the opportunity to speak before these two distinguished subcommittees. In keeping with your request, I would like to address the challenges Israel faces: security, conflict with the Palestinians and the de-legitimization movement.

Today, Israel is facing many security challenges, in an evolving threat environment. Between 1948 and 1973, the Arab-Israel conflict witnessed several state to state wars between neighbors. At least in those wars, states had rules of warfare. In the Arab-Israel context, these wars were classic pitched tank battles in the Sinai Desert or the Golan Heights. As such, for the most part, the fronts were not adjacent to urban areas. In contrast, today, Israel is encircled largely by non-state actors, which have no rules. They do not accept that Israel has a right to exist within any boundaries and critically, they aim to set the front line inside Israel's urban areas. They have no problem to embed themselves in the heart of urban areas, fire rockets into Israeli cities and in so doing, challenge Israel to retaliate in a terrain that could lead to greater civilian casualties on the Palestinian side.

On five of Israel's borders, Israel is facing non-state actors. First, in Lebanon, the dominant non-state actor is Hezbollah, which is believed to have 150,000 rockets. Second, along the Syrian border, where Syrian soldiers and UN peacekeepers once stood, there is now Jabhat al-Nusra, an offshoot of al-Qaeda. This does not even count ISIS, which is in eastern Syria and has openly threatened Jordan, a key Israeli ally. Third, on the Egyptian front in the south, an ISIS affiliate has wreaked havoc in the Sinai, territory ostensibly under Egyptian control since the 1979 Egyptian-Israeli peace treaty. This group is also trying to make inroads with Hamas in Gaza.

Fourth, there is Hamas in Gaza, which has fought three wars with Israel in the last seven-plus years, using the same formula of firing rockets at Israeli urban areas. The most recent war in 2014 lasted a full 51 days and civilians on both sides were impacted. Israelis had mere seconds to head for cover, hoping that Iron Dome missile defense debris would not land on their heads. Palestinian civilians also suffered tragic losses in relatively larger numbers due to Hamas' strategy of embedding fighters and weaponry in urban areas. And while today there is relative quiet along this front, it is only a matter of time before a fourth war begins in Gaza. Moreover, Hamas has resisted uniting Gaza under the Palestinian Authority. Needless to say, without US military assistance writ large and without Iron Dome specifically, Israel's security predicament would be far worse. A fifth border is a power-sharing arrangement with the Palestinian Authority in the West Bank, which I will discuss below.

The only border that resembles a classic state to state security relationship is that between Israel and Jordan. These are two states that have drawn much closer to each other in recent years amid shared threats and common interests.

Of course, beyond the challenges of its immediate neighbors, there is also Iran. Israel may not like the Iran deal, as we all know, but it understands it must now turn towards enhancing the US-Israel bilateral security relationship. At a joint conference with Secretary of Defense Ash Carter in October, Israeli Defense Minister Moshe Ya'alon said "The Iran deal is a given...Our disputes are over. And now we have to look to the future." Israel's military Chief of Staff, Gadi Eizenkot, even argued recently that in the short-term Israel is safer, given that the Iran nuclear deal forces the Iranians to ship out its stockpile of enriched uranium and cut down many of its centrifuges. Yet, two sets of questions remain. One is about what will happen when the restrictions on Iranian enrichment and deployment of advanced centrifuges are lifted under the terms of the deal over the next 10-15 years? Israel questions Washington's resoluteness to address the myriad of implementation issues that could arise. It also questions US willingness to ensure that Iran understands the consequences of dashing for the bomb, either during the agreement or after its main components expire. Second, in the more immediate sense, Israel worries that Iran is shedding its pariah status and will use access to post-sanctions capital to gain greater regional influence.

This rather sober assessment is punctuated by two rather unusual rays of light. First, despite the political impasse on peace negotiations since the collapse of Secretary of State John Kerry's initiative in 2014, Israeli-Palestinian security cooperation in the West Bank has, for the most part, been strong. Of course, nothing is ever easy and Palestinians control or partially control only 40% of the West Bank. There have been over 200 stabbings by Palestinians since October, many of them perpetuated by teenagers. While it is true that inflammatory statements by Mahmoud Abbas in the early days of this "lone wolf" stabbing wave exacerbated tensions, Israeli officials say PA security cooperation with Israel has been essential in ultimately reducing the violence. Israeli officials corroborate a statement by Palestinian Intelligence chief Majid Faraj to Defense News in January that the Palestinian security services have stopped 200 additional attacks. They also corroborate a recent statement by Abbas that the Palestinian security services have gone into Palestinian schools and confiscated knives. It is also known that Palestinian plainclothes police have stayed on the Palestinian side of key checkpoints to confiscate more knives and stop even more attacks. Israeli Defense Minister Moshe Ya'alon just last week held a press conference and praised the Palestinian security services for all their efforts against terrorism. He said "the PA has worked tirelessly recently to stop terror."

In return, Israel's security services have served an important stabilizing role within the Israeli structure and promoted further economic and security cooperation with the Palestinians. Officials say 120,000 Palestinians work in Israel or for Israelis in the West Bank and unofficial estimates are even higher. Since the start of the latest round of violence, the Israeli defense establishment has advocated for increasing this number by 30,000. The Israeli security services have also been advocates for providing the Palestinian security services with more authority in Palestinian urban areas (known as Area A). Such authority is premised upon more intelligence sharing, so Israel can avoid incursions, which have negative political implications for the PA. Israel insists that its forays into Palestinian urban areas are used sparingly, namely only when the intelligence is too sensitive to be shared with Palestinian counterparts. While Palestinians would like Israel to announce that it will stop all incursions in area A, in reality, both sides understand the Palestinians will need to gradually build capacity. Such a gradualist approach is in interest of both sides. Anything abrupt could set up the Palestinian side for failure.

In recent months, there has been a decline in violence and as of this writing, it is unclear who perpetrated yesterday's bus bombing in Jerusalem, the first in several years. In a preliminary sense, this decline seems to show that the Israeli security services have been vindicated in their approach. They have consistently argued against over-reaction, seeking to maintain an even-keel and avoid collective punishment of the Palestinian population. But it still may be too soon to pronounce the wave of stabbings over, as there could be an upsurge during the upcoming Jewish and Muslim holiday season. When I testified last time about clashes on the Temple Mount (TM), as it is known to Jews, and Haram al-Sharif (HAS), as it is known to Muslims, it was on the heels of the fall holiday season. During this time, Secretary Kerry, Jordan's King Abdullah and Israel's Prime Minister Netanyahu agreed on a camera system to ensure better security monitoring of the area. However, according to media reports, this plan has been abandoned amid Palestinian complaints. I hope it will be reinstated.

A second ray of hope for Israel, beset by non-state actors and a hegemonic Iran, is its growing cooperation with Sunni Arab states in the region. Israel has grown closer to Amman over fears that ISIS could infiltrate Jordan, a country Israel considers its strategic depth in the Mideast. Israel has been pulled closer to Egypt over fears about infiltrations of Hamas and the Sinai affiliate of ISIS. It is no secret that Israel is not enforcing the military restrictions for the Sinai, laid out in the 1979 Peace Treaty, when it comes to Egypt's fight against the ISIS affiliate. The idea that an Egyptian military jetliner would fly through Sinai with tacit Israeli acceptance would have been unfathomable in the past.

Israel has also been pulled closer to virtually all the six Gulf States, amid the shared fear of Iranian encroachment in the region. While these under-the-radar relations tend to focus on security and counter-terrorism, every once in a while they have protruded above the surface. In November, it was announced that Israel would establish a diplomatic mission to the International Renewable Energy Agency in the UAE, marking the first official Israeli presence in the Gulf in more than a decade. There is also the recent announcement signed between Egypt and Saudi Arabia, returning the islands of Tiran and Sanafir to Saudi sovereignty. Saudi Foreign Minister Adel al Jubeir said recently, "here is an agreement and commitments that Egypt accepted related to these islands, and the kingdom is committed to these," alluding to Saudi's first public recognition of the historic 1978 Camp David accords and the peace treaty that followed.

There have been two recent developments that are also worth noting. First is the Arab League's recent designation of Hezbollah as a terrorist organization. Second, just this past weekend, The Organization of Islamic Countries issued a statement which "deplored Iran's interference in the internal affairs of the States of the region and other Member States including Bahrain, Yemen, Syria, and Somalia, and its continued support for terrorism." Both these developments point to a Middle East that is more willing to publicly identify extremist threats. Often in the past, ambiguous phrasing was used to avoid ruffling feathers, unless the feathers ruffled were Israeli feathers. This is no longer the case.

What can the US do to tackle these threats and seize the opportunities?

When it comes to Iran, the US and Israel need to strictly enforce Iranian compliance of the nuclear deal and push back against malign Iranian behavior in the region. There needs to be consequences for violations, such as the recent missile tests. The US and Israel should form a joint implementation committee, which would deal with implementing the Joint Comprehensive Plan of Action, addressing potential violations and the maintenance and strengthening of non-nuclear sanctions. The US and Israel should also work together to track Iranian financial flows and Iranian arms transfers to Hezbollah.

The Iranian nuclear deal has triggered a wave of US arms commitments to the Gulf States, in order to offset the impact of the JCPOA. For Israel, this represents a tight-wire move. On one hand, Israel fears the possibility of sophisticated American hardware ending up in the wrong hands, as has been the case with ISIS in Iraq. At the same time, Israel itself is drawing closer to the Gulf States. In this context, the US has been and must continue to be committed to Israel's Qualitative Military Edge.

In a broad sense, Israel views the strength of the US-Israel relationship as a function of how the US is perceived in the region by friend and foe alike. If governments believe the US is trying to extricate itself from the Mideast, both the US and Israel will be deemed as having less credibility in the region. However, if the US is viewed as the center of the pragmatic camp in the Mideast, this will bolster the position of this critical bilateral relationship, at a time when Iranian proxies are involved in many of the region's conflicts.

Another way of bolstering the US-Israel security relationship is by concluding the Memorandum of Understanding (MOU), which sets foreign military aid levels for the next ten years. We have seen two MOUs in this regard in the last two decades. Concluding these negotiations swiftly will send a message to Israel's friends and enemies alike that the U.S. remains committed to Israel's security. Specifically, Israel's deterrent power is, in large part, a reflection of how its adversaries view the strength of its strategic relationship with Washington. An inability to conclude terms of an MOU satisfactory to both sides will erode this deterrence.

Of course, there are many steps that the US is already taking to bolster Israel's security, such as the ongoing development of missile defense technology. Today, the US is working with Israel on Arrow III and David's Sling. There is also the success of Iron Dome. Without Iron Dome, there would have been thousands of more fatalities in the 2014 Gaza War. Without Iron Dome giving Israel political breathing space, there is no doubt that Israel would have been forced into a ground assault, which would have increased both Israeli and Palestinian fatalities. There has also been closer technological cooperation in areas such as tunnel detection, preventing armed smuggling and cyber security. Israel sees itself as a leader in cyber-security and leading officials in the US have publicly said they see such cooperation as good for the US and something the US wants to intensify for its own interests.

On the Palestinian issue, there remain challenges. The US has engaged in three noble efforts in 2000, 2007/8, and 2013/2014 to solve the entire conflict. (As I have disclosed, I was part of the third.) For a variety of reasons, these efforts did not succeed and under the current leadership constellation, I don't see us succeeding in reaching a final deal. As such, I am rather skeptical about efforts to put forward parameters at the United Nations Security Council. Invariably a parameters resolution will be interpreted by both sides as an imposed solution and could serve as a baseline for defiance, rather than bringing the parties closer to a common solution. Moreover, I have my doubts that the US could reach a sufficiently explicit and balanced text, with equally tangible benefits, given the competing interests of the Security Council members. Taken together, I am concerned that a resolution will be seen as a walk-away strategy by the United States that ties the hands of future US administrations. We need more flexibility, not less in dealing with this complex issue.

Whenever it is all or nothing in the Middle East, it is always nothing. Therefore, we need to find a way to maintain the viability of a two-state outcome, even if we cannot implement a two-state solution today. I worry that stagnation will lead to further violence. Moreover, without a deal, Israel becomes a binational state, in contrast to Israel's desired identity as the nation-state of the Jewish people, albeit with equal rights for all citizens.

We have tried to hit the home-run ball three times, so perhaps now it is time for singles and doubles. It is important to note that approximately 80 percent of the Jewish settlers live in five percent of the West Bank, west of the security barrier. For Israel, this distribution of demography could be the key to maintaining the viability of a two-state solution. Israel could declare that it is not building east of the barrier, an area where a minority of settlers live but where the bulk of Palestinians reside, and consider financial incentives for settlers east of the barrier to move west. Israel could also announce that it will not build in Arab neighborhoods of East Jerusalem. This would focus Israeli activity largely into the small percentage area of the West Bank that Palestinians acknowledge will one day be Israel, in return for comparable territorial exchanges or swaps. Palestinian polls say an increasing number of Palestinians believe Israel will keep taking more of West Bank territory. Therefore, these steps could be an important signal to both Palestinians and the international community that Israel is serious about two states. This approach could help blunt the delegitimization movement, stem Israel's drift towards binationalism, give the US more leverage to block future Europeans sanctions against Israel and help improve the US-Israel relationship.

There are also moves the Palestinians can take to prove their commitment to two states. First, the Palestinian Authority could jettison its anti-normalization policy. It is hard to see how peace can be reached without a pro-active policy that encourages grassroots activity for reconciliation. Second, the Palestinians need to stop incentivizing terror by paying money to Palestinian prisoners and relatives of suicide bombers. This is not a small sum of money. Estimates put it at about $115 million per year. It is true that in 2014 the PA eliminated the Prisoner Affairs Ministry and the issue is now under the jurisdiction of the technically independent PLO. Yet, people continue to wonder if this is a sleight of a hand, since Abbas is the head of both and the PLO does not advertise the sources of its income.

Today, Abbas seems to be of two minds. On one hand, he will still call Palestinians stabbers who are killed "shahids" or "martyrs," even while indicating the action itself is not to be encouraged. He recently told an Israeli interviewer, "Our security forces go into the schools to search pupils' bags and see if they have knives…In one school, we found 70 boys and girls who were carrying knives. We took the knives and spoke to them and said: 'This is a mistake. We do not want you to kill and be killed. We want you to live, and for the other side to live as well.'"

The US also needs to sensitize our Europeans allies to this issue. When Europeans come to the US or perhaps when members of the US Congress go to Europe, it needs to be conveyed the Palestinians cannot continue to promote the message that terrorism pays and those that die stabbing Israelis are martyrs. Given the closeness between Europe and the Palestinians, this would carry weight. The Europeans love it when the US administers tough love to Israel in a public fashion, but they seem never to do the same when it comes to our Palestinian friends.

There is also the issue of the Boycott Divestment and Sanctions (BDS) movement. Sadly, the BDS movement is importing the politics of confrontation from the Middle East, rather than exporting the politics of pluralism and dialogue, which are the hallmarks of American society. As someone who has made scores of visits to American campuses since 2008, I am troubled by this movement for a variety of reasons. First, it puts the onus for the impasse entirely on Israel. As someone who was in the US Government, I can say this is definitely not accurate. On all three final status attempts, Israel has been willing to yield the land in question, if they know the deal will make them more secure, not more vulnerable. Second, there is the false perception that BDS is about using financial leverage to achieve an equitable two state solution. Omar Barghoutti, founder of BDS, has said he doesn't want Israel to exist at all. I continue to be troubled that the main group pursuing BDS on American campuses, called Students for Justice in Palestine (SJP), pointedly refuses to accept the idea of two states. I challenge SJP to disavow this policy and accept the principle of two states. Third, we must work to find an approach that creates wide-ranging coalitions on campus, involving Jewish and Muslim groups together. These divisive BDS resolutions rip campus communities apart. Instead, we must strive for practical coexistence. If the BDS movement is not blunted and there is no movement on the ground, along the lines I have suggested, I am concerned that this movement could metastasize beyond college campuses.

In conclusion, there are definite challenges, but there are also opportunities amid the crises. The dynamism of the US-Israel relationship will be tested by how our countries work together to meet these new challenges and in so doing, take our relationship to the next level.

Mr. POE. Thank you very much.

Dr. Wittes.

STATEMENT OF TAMARA COFMAN WITTES, PH.D., DIRECTOR, CENTER FOR MIDDLE EAST POLICY, BROOKINGS INSTITUTION

Ms. WITTES. Thank you, Mr. Chairman, Madam Chairman, Mr. Keating and Mr. Deutch, members of the committee.

I appreciate the invitation to appear before you and I must emphasize, as always, that I represent only myself before you because the Brookings Institution does not take any positions on policy issues.

On the afternoon following a day Israelis began with the discovery of yet another Hamas tunnel from Gaza into Israel, and that ended with the bombing of a bus, it seems like a very apt and sobering opportunity to give you some thoughts on the threats facing Israel from terrorism and from the impact of regional disorder.

I've had the chance to discuss these concerns with a range of Israeli officials and experts in the last several months, and I'll share my impressions with you.

Let me begin with Iran. When I appeared before you just about a year ago, I said that whether or not there was a nuclear deal, I thought we would see a more aggressive approach by Iran in a host of arenas around the region, where the upheaval has given them greater opportunities than before, and indeed, that's what we've seen.

Iran, helped in Syria by Russia, has pushed forward assertively to advance its influence and strengthen its allies around the region. In my view, this escalation of Iran's attempts at subversion was inevitable with or without a nuclear agreement.

Iran never lacked motivation for its assertions of power. Iran's sanctions-induced economic hardship did not prevent the country from spending billions supporting Assad and Hezbollah.

The fact is that the Arab uprisings of 2011, the civil wars that emerged in their wake and the sectarian narratives employed by Iran and its Arab adversaries have all given the Islamic Republic unprecedented opportunity to expand its activities and it has exploited these opportunities very successfully.

The main driver of instability and threat in the Middle East today is the civil violence that we see in Syria, Yemen, Libya and, increasingly, Iraq.

Ending those civil wars and the opportunities they create for bad actors should be a top priority for the United States and others concerned with regional stability.

The nuclear agreement with Iran is a concrete rollback of Iranian capability and IDF Chief of Staff Gadi Eizenkot noted in January that it abates for a period of time what had been Israel's greatest and most urgent security threat, and this gives the IDF important breathing space in which to focus on building its capabilities to address other threats and opportunities.

In Syria, the scenario that most concerns Israel is one in which Assad remains in power in Damascus and dependent on Iran for survival. Israeli officials also worry that continued chaos in Syria could allow jihadi groups like Jabhat al-Nusra or the Islamic State to launch attacks into Israel from the Golan.

But Israel's greatest concern is the impact of the Syrian war on Hezbollah for three reasons. First: Hezbollah's investment in saving Assad has altered the political equation in Lebanon in ways that could destabilize that country and motivate Hezbollah to try and win political points domestically by attacking Israel.

Second: The prospect of an outcome from the Syrian war that leaves Assad in power and Iran in effective control presages further transfers of weapons and technology from Iran to Hezbollah through Damascus. That is why the possibility of a negotiated settlement leaving Assad in power is such a concerning outcome for Israel.

Third: The Syrian war has given Hezbollah fighters extensive experience in conventional warfare, increasing their battle hardiness and capabilities in the event of another conflict with Israel.

A few comments on Hamas and Gaza—while Hamas has rebuilt, apparently, some of its tunnel and rocket capabilities since the 2014 conflict, current events suggest that it's still more interested right now in survival than in confrontation.

But should Hamas provoke another round with Israel, there's no question that the IDF would face many of the same military challenges that it faced in 2014.

Indeed, fighting terrorism in a heavily populated environment is a long-term challenge for the IDF whether in Gaza or, potentially, southern Lebanon or even, potentially, the West Bank. So building up new tactics and new capabilities against this challenge is a key task for Israel's military.

The situation in the West Bank is in many ways more volatile. My colleague has addressed it. What I will say is that the Palestinian Authority and Palestinian politics are not immune from the governance challenges faced by other Arab states.

There's a wide and growing gap between the Palestinian leadership and the public, particularly young people who see little prospect for economic, diplomatic or political progress in their current circumstances.

This points to the fact that the stalemate in the Israeli-Palestinian conflict carries a continuing cost for both sides. The status quo is deteriorating, not static, and reminds us that a negotiated resolution of this conflict remains Israel's best option for long-term security.

Finally, a word about ISIS in Sinai. The most recent statistics from the Taqrir Institute recorded 74 attacks against Egyptian targets in just the last quarter of 2015. That's nearly one every day.

Egypt's counter terrorism campaign in Sinai has been of limited impact. One Israeli source told me that the Egyptian campaign was mostly good at making the sand jump.

The Obama administration, as you know, is redirecting U.S. military assistance to Egypt away from long-term commitments to major weapons systems toward a focus on effective counter terror and border security. This is an effort that deserves the robust support of Congress.

Changes in the region have shifted the nature of the threats facing Israel, and from a broader perspective the decline for now of traditional state-based threats offers two opportunities for Israel—first, time and space to undertake longer-term planning for the structure, size, and capabilities of the IDF to meet the challenges ahead, and second, and perhaps more importantly, to seize the moment to determine what Israel wants in its future relationship with the Palestinians and push forward with steps to achieve a two-state solution that is in Israel's interest.

As the U.S. and Israel continue their discussions on a new 10-year MOU, it's important to evaluate the shift in Israel's threat environment and help Israel prepare accordingly.

Thank you.

[The prepared statement of Ms. Cofman Wittes follows:]

Israel's Changing Threat Environment

Testimony before the House Foreign Affairs Committee
Joint Hearing of the Subcommittee on Terrorism, Nonproliferation and Trade and the
Subcommittee on the Middle East and North Africa
by
Tamara Cofman Wittes
Senior Fellow and Director, Center for Middle East Policy
The Brookings Institution

April 19, 2016

Members of the Committee, thank you for the invitation to appear before you today. I am delighted to offer my views. I must emphasize, as always, that I represent only myself before you today; the Brookings Institution does not take any institutional positions on policy issues.

About a year ago, I appeared before this committee to discuss the likely impact on the region of a nuclear deal with Iran. On the afternoon following a day Israelis began with the discovery of yet another Hamas tunnel from Gaza into Israel, and that ended with the bombing of a bus, it seems like a very pat, and a very sobering opportunity to give you some thoughts on the threats facing Israel from terrorism and the impact of regional disorder. I've had the chance to discuss these concerns with a range of Israeli officials and experts in the last several months, and I'll share my impressions with you.

Let me begin with Iran, the government whose policies and proxies lie behind some of the worst threats Israel faces today. When I appeared before you last year, I said that "Whether there's a nuclear deal or not, I predict we will see a more aggressive approach by Iran in a host of arenas around the region, where the upheaval has given them greater opportunities than before." And indeed that's what we've seen — Iran, helped in Syria by Russia, has pushed forward assertively to advance its influence and strengthen its allies around the region. The Iranian threat — not primarily the threat of nuclear capabilities but rather these other dimensions of Iranian behavior destabilizing the region — has led Israel and the Sunni Arab states of the region to find more common ground in the past year than perhaps ever before.

That said, I want to emphasize that in my view this escalation of Iran's attempts at subversion around the region was inevitable with or without a nuclear agreement. While sanctions relief will, over time, give the Iranian government more resources, the Islamic Republic has been committed to this path since 1979. Ever since this revolutionary regime was established, it has sought to exploit the cracks within societies across the region to expand its own influence. Iran never lacked motivation for its assertions of power. Iran's sanctions-induced economic hardship did not prevent them from giving Hezbollah hundreds of millions of dollars a year, or prevent them from spending billions of dollars and their own soldiers' lives keeping Bashar al-Assad in power. The Arab uprisings of 2011, the civil wars that emerged in their wake, and the sectarian narratives employed by Iran and its Arab adversaries have all given Iran unprecedented opportunities to expand its activities, and it has exploited those opportunities very successfully. So yes, Iranian interference across the region is likely to continue in the wake of the Iran deal — and it was getting worse with or without the deal. The main driver of instability and threat in the Middle East today is the civil violence in Syria, Yemen, Libya, and increasingly in Iraq. Ending those civil wars should be a top priority for the United States and others concerned with regional stability.

In a major speech in January outlining Israel's strategic environment, IDF chief of staff Gadi Eisenkot noted that the P5+1 nuclear agreement with Iran is a turning point for Israel, because the nuclear threat from Iran used to be the biggest threat Israel faced. While Israel does not assume that Iran will fully comply with the deal, Eisenkot recognized that the dismantling of centrifuges and the Arak reactor, and the shipment of uranium out of the country, have concretely rolled back Iran's nuclear capabilities. He also noted that the IDF does believe that Iran will work hard over the coming five years to gain the advantages they will get by complying with the terms of the agreement. Indeed, Eisenkot said that he did not anticipate Israel facing major nonconventional weapons threats in the near future, because the nuclear deal has rolled back Iran's nuclear capabilities and put them under tighter controls, and because of the removal of chemical weapons from Syria. That gives the IDF important breathing space in which to focus on building up capabilities to address other threats and opportunities. Let me address now some of these other threats.

Syria

For the first several years of the war in Syria, Israel took a fairly hands-off approach: concerned over the emergence of jihadi groups, but wary of Hezbollah and Iranian involvement backing Assad. Israelis used to see the Syrian government as a stable and predictable adversary, and even sometimes as a check on Iran and Hezbollah. But today Israeli military officials judge that it's unlikely Bashar will again control all of Syrian territory, and they see him as dependent and subservient within the Syrian-Iranian alliance.

As a result, it's clear today that the scenario that most concerns Israel in Syria is one in which Assad remains in power in Damascus, and remains dependent on Iran for survival — leaving Iran with stronger influence on Israel's northern border than it had before the war. Iran is determined to sustain Assad in power because Syria is the strategic depth and channel of support to Hezbollah, Iran's most effective regional ally, and is also a good entry point for Iran to the Arab-Israeli arena. According to a new BBC investigation and other sources, Iran has reportedly bolstered its IRGC forces in Syria with militias made up of Iraqi Shia and of Hazara refugees from Afghanistan, who are picked up in Iran and given minimal training before being sent to Syria to fight. The level of Iranian investment in Assad's survival is impressive, and should increase our skepticism that the diplomatic talks including Iran will yield a constructive outcome. Israeli officials also worry that continued chaos in Syria, should the war continue unabated or escalate, could allow jihadi groups like Jabhat al-Nusra and Islamic State to launch attacks into Israel from the Golan. Israel will be looking to the United States, and to some extent the Sunni Arab states who share its concern over Assad and Iran, to advance its interests in the diplomatic talks.

Hezbollah

Of even greater concern to Israel is the impact of the Syrian war on Hezbollah. That concern has several dimensions.

First, Hezbollah's investment in saving Assad has altered the political equation in Lebanon in ways that could destabilize the country. Hezbollah fighters have been operating in Syria, perhaps about 5000 at a time in rotation, and they have lost about a thousand fighters there. This emphasizes very clearly for all to see (including the Lebanese people) that the organization is not so focused, as it claims, in defending Lebanon, but rather on increasing its own power and influence and securing Shia and Iranian influence in the Arab world. In addition, the Syrian civil war has spilled over into Lebanon already, reigniting sectarian tensions and generating an influx of one million Syrian refugees – that's adding 25% to Lebanon's population. The tensions in Lebanon are evident in its politics – the sect-based political factions have been unable to agree on a president for the past year and a half. Hezbollah has been boycotting parliament as well, exercising its effective veto over the political system, and preventing any progress on basic governance in the country. If sectarian tension in Lebanon increases, and particularly if Sunni extremist groups fired up by the Syrian war carry out more violent attacks in Lebanon, Hezbollah could easily choose to try and win political points domestically by attacking Israel. Thus far, Hezbollah has not chosen this path, perhaps because of Israel's deterrent power, perhaps because it worries about overstretch fighting on two fronts; but one cannot assume that reticence will last forever, and unintended escalation is also a possibility.

Second, the prospect of an outcome from the Syrian war that leaves Assad in power and Iran in effective control of the country presages further transfers of weapons and technology from Iran to Hezbollah through Damascus. Iran has already enabled Hezbollah to expand its rocket and missile arsenal to nearly 100,000, some with advanced guidance and some with range that would enable them to target infrastructure and to reach all of Israel's population centers. This prospect makes leaving Assad in control of Damascus a deeply concerning outcome for Israel's security. Israel has acted to try and prevent the transfer of advanced technology to Hezbollah through Damascus several times over the course of the Syrian conflict — but 100% success would be a miracle.

Third, the Syrian war has given Hezbollah fighters extensive experience in conventional warfare, increasing their battle hardiness and thus their capabilities in the event of another war with Israel. Should Hezbollah embark on a campaign of rocket attacks on Israeli territory, the scope of the threat would likely lead Israel to move quickly toward a ground offensive in southern Lebanon designed to reduce or eliminate the attacks. But as Eisenkot noted in January, Hezbollah has scattered its presence across 240 villages in southern Lebanon; each has a defense system; and each, of course, also has a civilian population. In the event of a new confrontation, Israel will be facing a more entrenched, more experienced enemy and the IDF will face real dilemmas in ground operations in southern Lebanon.

Hamas in Gaza

Iran continues to seek to provide funding and weapons to Hamas and Palestine Islamic Jihad in Gaza. While Hamas has reportedly rebuilt some of its tunnel and rocket capabilities since the 2014 conflict, it has not so far sought a new confrontation with Israel. Rather, the rocket attacks from Gaza in 2015 were launched by salafi groups in the Strip that are seeking to compete with and displace Hamas; and Hamas has dealt with them harshly. Recent reports suggest that, under pressure from Cairo, Hamas is also trying to sever links to Sinai militants and prevent its own operatives from going into Sinai. In other words, current events indicate that Hamas seems more interested right now in survival in power, than in confrontation with Israel.

Should Hamas provoke another round with Israel, there is no question that the IDF would face many of the same challenges militarily that it faced in 2014 — in terms of the threat from tunnels, and in terms of the way Hamas embedded both fighters and weapons within the civilian population. Indeed, fighting terrorism in a heavily populated environment is a long-term challenge for the IDF, whether in Gaza or potentially in southern Lebanon or the West Bank. Building up new tactics and capabilities against this challenge is a key task for Israel's military in the coming years.

The West Bank and the "Knife Intifada"

The wave of violence that began in September last year has comprised hundreds of attacks, and claimed the lives of several dozen Israelis, over two hundred Palestinians, and several Americans. According to public comments by officials, the IDF and security services understand this violence to be of a different nature than past terrorism by Palestinians. The attacks do not, for the most part, appear to be directed by any organization, and the individuals who carry out these attacks often do not seem to have planned the attacks in advance in any meaningful way. The lack of organization or direction means that there is little tactical warning that Israel's security forces can use to prevent these attacks; they can only react.

According to the briefings I received in January, the incitement that was evident in the Palestinian media and in politicians' statements in the early months has been significantly reduced, and the IDF was expecting a reduction in the overall number of attacks due to increased efforts both by Israel and by the Palestinian Authority. This past month has seen a dramatic drop in the number of attacks. Two weeks ago, Palestinian Authority President Mahmoud Abbas gave a notable interview to Ilana Dayan of Israel's Channel Two in which he condemned the violence in robust terms and called on Palestinians to stop these attacks. He acknowledged the problem of incitement in the Palestinian media, and spoke powerfully about his security forces' coordination with Israel to prevent attacks. He also reiterated that he sees Netanyahu as a peace partner and is prepared to meet with him at any time.

Overall, Israeli security sources say clearly that the drivers for those who carry out these attacks include despair at the lack of any political horizon in the conflict with Israel. This points to the fact that the stalemate in the Israeli-Palestinian conflict carries a continuing cost for both societies, and that cost may be increasing over time. The status quo in this conflict is deteriorating, not static, and reminds us that a negotiated resolution of the conflict remains Israel's best option for long-term security.

The Israeli government has sought to avoid responding to the attacks in ways that severely constrain the wider Palestinian population. For example, throughout this wave of attacks, 120,000 Palestinians have continued to work inside Israel and in Israeli settlements in the West Bank. The Israeli government has also sought to bolster the Palestinian economy in other ways. These steps are directed toward stabilizing a shaky Palestinian Authority which is a crucial bulwark for Israel against instability and inroads by radical groups into the West Bank.

Palestinian politics are not immune from the governance challenges faced by other Arab societies. There is a wide and growing gap between the Palestinian leadership and the public, particularly young people who see little prospect for economic, diplomatic, or political progress in their current circumstances. Continued uncertainty about leadership succession in the Palestinian Authority and the Palestinian national movement more generally also raises concern over a potential weakening or collapse of PA security forces. Israeli officials I spoke to expressed concern that the anger and violence currently directed against Israel would, if it continues, inevitably turn against the Palestinian Authority as well; and that could provoke a collapse of the PA or an end to Israel-PA security cooperation. This could leave the IDF feeling pressured to reenter Palestinian population centers in an ongoing way, and could make the West Bank vulnerable to inroads by ISIS and other radical groups.

Sinai and ISIS's Egyptian Affiliate

The ISIS affiliate in Sinai has continued to attack Egyptian targets nearly every day. The most recent statistics from the Tahrir Institute, which tracks terrorism in Egypt, recorded 74 attacks in the last quarter of 2015. These included the downing of a Russian passenger plane on October 31st, which has devastated what was left of Egypt's tourist economy. ISIS has also claimed assassination attempts against government officials and individuals accused of supporting the government, IEDs, and armed assaults on various military and civilian facilities.

Egypt's counterterrorism campaign in Sinai has been of limited impact in reducing attacks; one Israeli source told me that the Egyptian campaign was mostly good as "making the sand jump." There are concerns among some observers both in Israel and here in Washington that the Egyptian military's tactics may even be counterproductive. Egypt has, for example, razed homes along the Sinai border with Israel, destroying farmland and displacing thousands of Sinai residents. Such tactics may be alienating Sinai residents and giving ISIS more room to operate. Similarly, Egypt's overcrowded jails are reportedly hotbeds for extremist recruitment.

The Obama Administration, as you know, is redirecting US military assistance to Egypt away from long-term commitments to major weapons systems, and toward effective counterterror and border security capabilities. This effort deserves the robust support of Congress. The United States also has both legal and moral obligations to ensure that its support for Egyptian counterterror efforts does not contribute to human rights abuses, which have vastly escalating in the last two years in Egypt. I know this is an issue your committee is watching closely.

Conclusions

It's clear that the changes in the region have shifted the nature of the threats facing Israel — from state-centered and nonconventional threats to non-state, terrorist and insurgent threats. Israel has long relied on deterrence and superior military capabilities as the backbone of its defense. But the new threat profile challenges that approach. As General Eisenkot has asked, how does one deter terrorist organizations that are not accountable to anyone? Likewise, overwhelming conventional military capabilities are better suited for a major land war than for a campaign against a terrorist group that is embedded within a civilian population.

From a broader perspective, there is in fact a sort of "threat trough" for Israel at the present moment, which presents important strategic opportunities. Iran is pre-occupied with its geopolitical competition with the Sunni Arab states, and its nuclear program has been rolled back in concrete terms, taking that threat off the table for a period of years. Some of Israel's worst enemies in previous years – Syria, Iraq, and Libya – are consumed by civil war themselves. Hamas has less Iranian support than in the past, and is contained and reticent after its 2014 confrontation with Israel; and Hezbollah is for now wholly committed in Syria.

Two opportunities emerge for Israel from this changed threat environment: first, time and space to undertake longer-term planning for the structure, size, and capabilities of the Israel Defense Forces to meet the challenges ahead, especially from non-state actors. Second and perhaps more importantly, to seize the moment to determine what it wants in its future relationship with the Palestinians, and to push forward with steps to advance the two-state solution that Israel's leader continues to avow is in his country's best interests. This unique moment should not be wasted.

As the United and Israel continue discussions on a new ten-year memorandum of understanding on defense assistance, it will be important to evaluate this fundamental shift in Israel's threat environment and help Israel prepare accordingly. Enshrining US-Israel defense cooperation in a new MOU will help address emerging threats, and will give the IDF needed predictability in funding to implement its new long-term plans. Most of all, a new MOU will send a clear signal to adversaries and friends alike about the depth and breadth of the US-Israel defense partnership. In other words, the significance of the MOU goes well beyond a dollar amount, a specific capability, or a specific source of threat. I hope it will be concluded soon.

———

Mr. POE. Thank you, Dr. Wittes. I will recognize myself for questions.

These entities have been mentioned by the four of you all that are hostile toward Israel—Hezbollah, Hamas, Syria, Nusra Front, the Palestinians, ISIS and Iran, including the three organizations that are defunct—the Holy Land Foundation, the Kind Hearts—interesting name—Islamic Association for Palestine.

All of these groups do not like Israel. Some of them have publicly proclaimed "Death to the Israelis." But they have one thing in common—none of them like Israel.

What is one—what is the basis of that? Why are they hating on Israel for so many years, if I can use the phrase my grandkids use? One of you want to try to address that?

Dr. Rubin.

Mr. RUBIN. If I may, very briefly.

Mr. POE. Please.

Mr. RUBIN. It's possible to think about terrorism and the motivations for terrorism on a spectrum ranging from grievance on one side to ideology on the other. Our State Department across administrations tends to be addicted to the notion that terrorism is motivated by grievance and that can be very comforting because that means you can come up with some magic formula of incentives to make that terrorism go away.

We need to recognize much more directly the ideological basis of most terrorism that there is no magic formula, there is no concession—that ultimately what you have to do is delegitimize that ideology. We have done it before with the Baader-Meinhof Gang. We can do it now.

Mr. POE. Okay. Let's be a little more specific. You got Iran testing ballistic missiles and they put on the side in Hebrew "Death to Jerusalem" or "Death to Israel." Is this a religious phenomena philosophy that is uniting these organizations or is it not? What is the basis of the philosophy? Forget about the grievances. Center on the philosophy. What is the philosophy they all have in common, if they do have one in common?

Mr. SCHANZER. Mr. Chairman, I think it's safe to say that we're talking about militant Islam—radical Islam, whatever you'd like to call it. I know it's not a very popular term these days in Washington but it is a radical ideology that empowers both this—what we call the Sunni and Shi'a sides of the street.

You got the Islamic State. You've got the Islamic Republic. Their hatred for Israel, their Islamist ideology is what—is what really motivates the terrorism that they carry out.

This has been our battle since 9/11. We continue to battle it. It's taken on different forms in this town. But I think that the challenge still remains.

Mr. POE. So if we recognize it as for what it is—radical Islam opposed to Israel based on a philosophy—as opposed to a grievance, it's more difficult to deal with. Would you agree or not?

Mr. SCHANZER. Absolutely.

Mr. POE. All right. The IRGC, do you think that that should be labelled as a terrorist organization? Any of you think that it should?

Mr. MAKOVSKY. Yes, I absolutely do. Now, in Iran's both—in both Iran's constitution and in the founding statute of the Islamic Revolutionary Guard Corps, it defines the purpose of both the Islamic Republic and the Islamic Revolutionary Guard Corps as an export of revolution.

In 2008, in an internal Iranian debate this was defined exclusively as hard power in terms of sabotaging other countries basically with bombs and bullets.

Now, we oftentimes talk about the Iranian political spectrum from hardliner to reformist. You will note that American policy makers don't talk about the Islamic Revolutionary Guard Corps and the factual divisions therein in the same way, number one, because we don't have adequate intelligence on that, and number two, no matter what the Iranian people might think it's ultimately the guys with the guns that matter and the most ideologically pure members of these units are the ones that have the capabilities to attack Israel and the will to do so.

Mr. POE. The groups the Holy Land Foundation, the Kind Hearts, Islamic Association for Palestine—those were tax-exempt organizations that are now defunct, and there's a new organization in Chicago, the American Muslims for Palestine. Are some of the folks that were working with those groups that have been put out of business by the Treasury Department—have they moved over to this new organization and still doing the same thing?

Mr. SCHANZER. Mr. Chairman, we've identified in this testimony that we've got three individuals from Holy Land that have moved over to AMP.

Mr. POE. Let me interrupt because I just got a few minutes left—seconds left.

Is this a—this new organization is it a tax-exempt organization as well?

Mr. SCHANZER. So three from Holy Land, three from Islamic Association for Palestine, one from Kind Hearts all now working for AMP, which is pretty significant, we think, when we look at the leadership. When you——

Mr. POE. Are they raising money for any organization—terrorist organizations or do you know?

Mr. SCHANZER. Not that we know of. What we can tell you is that AMP is a corporate nonprofit. It has a 501(c)(3) that is its fiscal sponsor. So it raises tax deductible donations, passes them through what's known as AJP, Americans for Justice in Palestine. It passes through to AMP and then AMP then passes it on to campus. It's quite a structure.

Mr. POE. Thank you.

I yield to the gentleman from Massachusetts, Mr. Keating, the ranking member.

Mr. KEATING. Thank you, Mr. Chairman.

I was intrigued with Dr. Wittes' comments about Egypt and advanced weaponry. But I want to take that on a different tack if I can.

Last week, the Prime Minister—Prime Minister Netanyahu—announced that Israel launched a number of strikes inside Syria, targeting suspected arms transfers to Hezbollah fighters.

When I talked to the Prime Minister last year, he said—it's not surprising that he did that because he said unless something affects his borders he had no intention of doing that.

At the same time, Israel diplomatically reached out to Russia and wanted assurances that their weaponry, since they are departing the area without announcement, not fall into the hands of Iranians or, particularly, Hezbollah.

So there's a concern there. How much of a threat is that, is the weaponry falling into the hands of groups like Hezbollah. Mr. Makovsky.

Mr. MAKOVSKY. As far as I know, things like the SA-300, the SA-400 remain under Russian command and control. The Russians have not been sharing this weaponry with their—with the Syrian Government or anything. They insist on operating it themselves.

But I think what the Prime Minister, by the way, told you I think is accurate. I think that is—Israel has learned from 1982 it's very difficult to social engineer an Arab state, and they are more humble about the limits of their use of force than others may be about them and I think that they have limited their engagement in the Syria conflict to defense.

You know, if you fire and hit Israel, Israel will hit back. But if they also see advanced weaponry, and Netanyahu has now said publicly these have been dozens of times that they've detected advanced weaponry going from Hezbollah in Syria to Hezbollah in Lebanon, they're going to hit them. But it's pure defense at this point and I think they do not think they will be decisive in any way, shape, or form given the myriad of militias inside Syria and have taken in that sense a very low profile and very limited objectives.

Mr. KEATING. You also mentioned, though, at the same time, I believe, that Israel may enter the battlefield. Will those be instances where that weaponry is getting transferred? Is that your suggestion?

Mr. MAKOVSKY. As far as I know, those has been—and I've asked this to IDF and other security people when I was over there and they have a very limited kind of objective, which is advanced weaponry that's being transferred to Hezbollah in Lebanon.

Mr. KEATING. I think that's a real concern to be watchful from the U.S. standpoint. You know, the lone wolf attacks—that's something that represent the greatest risk to us here in the U.S. as well.

How much is that—could you comment on how social media is being used in those areas and what Israel might be doing to try and counter that, since it remains our greatest threat here at home as well?

Mr. MAKOVSKY. I'll just throw in—maybe my colleagues have thoughts. I talked to the premier Palestinian poster, Khalil Shikari—maybe known to some of you—based in Ramallah.

He told me 86 percent of Palestinian teenagers—probably no different than in this country, I should say—get their news from social media.

I see this as a huge issue, which is Arab social—Palestinian social media. We know a lot of 15-year-olds refer to their going on social media as—it might be the final trigger for them in terms of doing their lone wolf attacks.

Of course, there are deeper reasons, I'm sure. But I think it's very serious. I mean, it just—it's striking to me that the start-up nation of Israel that knows during the Gaza war if someone's on a fourth floor walk-up in Gaza and Israel has this knock on the roof program, which is you're on the fourth floor walk-up but Israel is going to tell you they're about to hit this building—go a few blocks away.

First of all, I don't know too many armies that would give such advance notice but Israel does it. But if they could find the kid on the fourth floor walk-up and send him a text message in Arabic during a war there's got to be a way to use this start-up nation to reach more conciliatory messages on—in Arabic media.

I think this is a real challenge and I think you're very correct in putting your finger on, I think, a key venue of this issue—effort against stabbings, which is need to work on the Arabic social media.

Mr. KEATING. Do you see anything with BDS and networking that surrounds that that could be also something of a threat to Israel in terms of beyond just their divesture attempts but other means of expanding that, that being a threat for itself?

I know in 16 states and localities there's already anti-BDS legislation but how effective has it been to date in terms of hurting Israel as well as do you see any way of collaboration with that effort and incorporating social media? I've left you 1 second. I'm sorry. Anything you could add.

Mr. MAKOVSKY. It should be said that BDS and with all these campus resolutions not a single American university has divested from Israel.

So sometimes we need to remember that as well, that it has not yet happened. But it's a question of a certain mood that's set, an effort to try to compare Israel to an old South Africa, to invoke some of these old campus battles, and I think the only way to compete with this——

I was just at Ohio State the night before a big BDS vote, meeting with Ohio State student senators and my approach, and people on this panel know me, is that the only way to, you know—the important thing is to do practical co-existence and there are a lot of organizations out there that does people to people.

I know there's a group here in Washington with an umbrella of, like, 90 different people-to-people groups. There's a need—students want to do practical co-existence.

I think you need to look for ways that bring campuses, student groups together and do not rip the community apart over something that is divisive, counter productive and just wrong.

And so I think we should be accentuating the positive rather than focusing, I mean, on the negative. You should warn against the negative but, you know, you should focus on things that could be effective in building bridges of co-existence.

There are a lot of groups out there that are doing that practical work and I think students that go on alternative spring breaks and other sorts of activities to do this can do it in this Israeli-Palestinian sector as well.

56

Mr. KEATING. Okay. Thank you.

Mr. POE. I thank the gentleman for his questions.

The Chair recognizes the gentlelady from Florida, the chairman of the Middle East Subcommittee, for her comments, questions and answers.

Ms. ROS-LEHTINEN. Thank you so much, Judge Poe.

Last week, our Middle East Subcommittee had Assistant Secretary Patterson and we asked her about the status of the MOU negotiations. She said this administration might not secure an agreement before the term is up and we're seeing reports just today that the administration is about to approve sales of fighter jets to Qatar and Kuwait which will, of course, worry the Israelis, as this is set to erode its qualitative military edge, and continued U.S. assistance to Israel is so critical to ensuring that the Jewish state can protect herself against the threats that we're talking about today, and I'm sure that many of you would agree that this sends a troubling signal to Israel and to those who seek to do her harm.

Those are the ones who really receive these signals and for us to preclude the MOU and have a strong MOU that would send a very strong message of support to Israel. So I hope that this administration does that, and maybe we'll talk about it if we have time.

But Dr. Schanzer, I wanted to give you an opportunity to elaborate on the great research that you have done. You mention in your testimony that Treasury has not made a domestic designation of a charity for supporting terrorism since 2009.

And we have all of these terror threats in our homeland and I find that surprising. You're looking into the financial networks of some domestic entities that operate in support of the BDS campaign, and I thank you for that.

What can you tell us about their donor networks and their corporate structure and what does it—what does it say to you about no new designations?

Do you think that Treasury has been successful in stopping illegal fundraising in the U.S. and that's why there have been no new designations?

Would you say that there seems to be a shift in U.S. policy from this administration in recent years and that makes it more difficult for our agencies to pursue domestic terrorism financing. And I'd like to give you the remaining time.

Mr. SCHANZER. Thank you, Madam Chairman.

On the question of Treasury designations, all I can tell you is anecdotally when I speak to former Treasury colleagues my understanding is that they don't look at these issues any longer. This may be something that is linked to this administration. It also could just be a shifting of the mission of Treasury.

So I think I would be careful to say that this is politically motivated. My understanding is that the FBI should and is still looking at domestic terror finance.

And so whenever we look at these illicit finance questions I think there's probably a team of people who should be looking at it. But I think it might be an interesting question to ask the Treasury whether this is still their mission or not.

As for the corporate structure of the groups that I talked about today, it's a very interesting structure in that there is a 501(c)(3) which is transparent. That's the Americans for Justice in Palestine.

They file 990s. They are the fiscal sponsor for this group AMP, which I described in detail today. AMP is a corporate nonprofit which it's my understanding that this is supposed to be a temporary status for an organization on its way to being a full 501(c)(3). They have not made that jump, and so I'm curious as to why they have not done so. And as I mentioned, AMP appears to be the organization that's giving a lot of the assistance to Students for Justice in Palestine, the campus-based groups.

They're the ones who hand the apartheid walls and they provide the speakers and printed material. They give a lot of guidance. They have a campus coordinator that works with SJP. So it's a very interesting corporate structure. I encourage you to take a look into that.

And then as for donor network, I can tell you that we have looked into it. I deliberately chose not to include it in our discussion today. As you know, the environment for Islamic charities has not been an easy one.

I think there are a lot of Muslim Americans out there who are very scared of contributing to charities that may be involved in terrorism. I didn't want to list them. I'm happy to provide them to you offline.

But the bottom line here, from my perspective, is is that when you look at an organization like AMP and they have individuals who have previously worked for charities that have either been designated by the U.S. Government, that they have been dissolved by the U.S. Government or found civilly liable in a Federal court, you would think that this would be something that they disclosed to their donors and I am not sure that they have done so. I think that that is a matter of significant concern.

Ms. ROS-LEHTINEN. That they're mandated to do or should they be mandated to do?

Mr. SCHANZER. It's my understanding that there is no watch list, so to speak, and I'm not suggesting that we have one. But I do think that disclosure of that past activity would be incredibly important to donors who are contributing to these charities so that they know what they're getting into.

They know that they could be running into problems later on down the line based on the past experiences of these individuals.

Ms. ROS-LEHTINEN. Thank you so much for such great research. Thank you, Mr. Chairman.

Mr. POE. The Chair recognizes the ranking member, Mr. Deutch from Florida.

Mr. CONNOLLY. Thanks, Mr. Chairman.

Dr. Wittes, you spoke about—you referenced the attacks against Egypt in your testimony and it's clear that Israel finds herself sharing many of the same security concerns as many of the Arab states in the neighborhood.

Are there ways—and the idea comes up from time to time—but are there tangible ways that these countries can work together to counter mutual threats, both Israel with those countries that—where there are peace agreements in place and perhaps even those countries where there are shared interests but not formal peace agreements?

Ms. WITTES. Absolutely, Congressman Deutch. I think that there are two key avenues and we see some activity along both these lines already underway.

The first is countering Iran and Iran's destabilizing activities around the region. This is the interest that has drawn Israel and a number of Arab states closer together over the past year than I think they have ever been before, and it's an interest that I think will be sustained into the future. It's not a short-term problem.

So there is a lot of quiet conversation and information sharing. What there is not is kind of overt cooperation along these lines. But since a lot of this Iranian activity is below the radar, that kind of information sharing can be absolutely crucial.

The second avenue is stabilizing key front line states and those include states that have peace treaties with Israel, most particularly Jordan but Egypt as well. We know, of course, the Gulf States have been important supporters financially and diplomatically and politically of both Jordan and Egypt and that is absolutely crucial for both of those governments. I think Israel continues to keep an eye on Jordanian stability. And then additionally, there is the question of diplomatic negotiations ending the civil war in Syria. Israel is not at the table. It's not in the room. But many of the Sunni Arab states are, and that's an additional opportunity for cooperation.

Mr. CONNOLLY. Thank you very much.

Mr. Makovsky, I want to return to your topic of tough love. There are some who might suggest that the Vice President's expression of overwhelming frustration with Israel might constitute tough love from the United States. Do you agree?

Secondly, if that is so, what is the kind of tough love that you would like to see by our European friends with respect to the Palestinians and, frankly, the kind of tough love that perhaps we should expect and administer her as well?

Mr. MAKOVSKY. Thank you, Congressman.

I want to be clear. By the way, on the last point about Ohio State, the BDS advocates lost the vote. So the anti-BDS forces won, if I didn't make that clear.

When I spoke about tough love, I was not talking as an advocate of it. I'm saying the same Europeans who call for tough love of the U.S. toward Israel are not willing to administer that when it comes to their own relations with the Palestinians. That was the context of my remarks.

For example, when the President of the United States delivered two speeches in May 2011 where he talked about returning to the '67 borders plus swaps land exchanges, there is no—there has not been an Obama speech equivalent out of Brussels or London or Berlin or Paris saying, and you Palestinians, when it comes to refugees you return to the state of Palestine, not to Israel. That would be very important if the Europeans would do that. Or if they would say that, you know, that the aid to families of suicide bombers is reprehensible or saying anti-normalization runs against the very spirit of peace—we want you to encourage more people-to-people exchanges.

These are things the Europeans can do that would make the difference, and whatever is not said publicly I am concerned will not be heard on the Palestinian side. I think the Europeans can—could say it but they've never been really prodded to do so.

Mr. CONNOLLY. Is there—is there an opportunity to prod—I throw this out to Dr. Rubin and Dr. Schanzer—is there an opportunity—wouldn't it be appropriate to prod the Europeans to do exactly that now, even as we work under the Iran nuclear deal to make it easier for them to develop additional business in Iran?

Not that—not that they're linked but given the successes that they're seeing under the nuclear deal the ability to make further investment in Iran and the way in which the deal—nuclear deal—encourages that, shouldn't we also be in a position to remind them that at the same time the threats that Iran poses in the region get in the way of peace, and also standing in the way of peace are the kinds of things that Mr. Makovsky just spoke about and it would be helpful for them to say that clearly?

Mr. SCHANZER. Congressman Deutch, I think there—that we have some frank discussions that we need to be having with the Europeans right now.

They're obviously very eager to reignite the financial relationships with Iranian businesses. First of all, and I think we've made this clear at FDD, that we are very concerned about the United States facilitating those through dollar transactions.

We have said time and again that this is not a good idea to allow Iran access to our financial system in any way despite the European request to do so and we think that it should be—we should continue to hold the line on that.

More broadly, I think the Europeans have not exactly played the role that we've looked for on the Iran deal or with regard to the Palestinian-Israeli conflict. The Europeans right now are mulling a resolution to pressure the Israelis through a multilateral decision-making process for how to solve the Palestinian-Israeli conflict.

I can't think of anything that would be more detrimental to Israel's long-term survivability than to have something akin to the P5+1 make a decision on how Israel should cede territory in the future to a state that is possibly not viable.

So I think these are the sorts of discussions that we need to be having with the Europeans both about Iran transactions as well as what they're doing at the U.N. Neither have been terribly productive.

Mr. CONNOLLY. Thank you very much. Thank you, Mr. Chairman.

Mr. POE. The Chair recognizes the gentleman from Texas, Mr. Weber.

Mr. WEBER. Thank you, Mr. Chairman.

Dr.—is it Schanzer? Is that how you say that? Earlier in your comments you said, I think, we've been battling with radical Islam since 9/11. What do you think about the prior attacks starting in '79, Yemen, the bombing of the Cole, the U.S. Marine barracks and I can go—the prior—I mean, what about those?

Mr. SCHANZER. You're absolutely right, Congressman Weber. I meant that we were—we've been battling over it in this country the debate over what to call it since 9/11. But in fact——

Well, some of us haven't been.

Mr. SCHANZER. Fair enough. But to your point, absolutely we've been dealing with radical Islam from the Islamic Republic since 1979——

Mr. WEBER. Okay. Okay.

Mr. SCHANZER [continuing]. The Muslim Brotherhood since the 1920s.

Mr. WEBER. I just want to make that point, and you can even go back further than that.

But Mr. Makovsky—is that how you say that? You also said that Israel learned, in your exchange with Bill Keating, in 1982 that they can't socially engineer an Arab state. Would you explain that?

Mr. MAKOVSKY. What I meant is 1982 Israel thought that it could decide who was going to be the next leader of Lebanon, a guy by the name of Bachir Gemayel, and that whole experience ended in calamity.

So I think they very—you know, in terms of their interest they are very keen in terms of where they could succeed and where they cannot succeed.

Mr. WEBER. Okay. I just—I'm sorry, I just wasn't familiar with that date. Didn't know what you were referring to. And then you also said Israel knocks on a roof in the social media battle.

You indicated that if they can find that 12-year-old kid on the fourth floor they should be able to—but I would offer that social media is a relatively new phenomenon in that—at that level—Twitter and all that stuff the last, I don't know, 2 or 3 years—I'm dating myself—maybe longer than that. But some of these kids get indoctrinated to hate Jews since the time they're two or three or younger. Is that accurate?

Mr. SCHANZER. Yes, that is accurate.

Mr. WEBER. So how do you combat that?

Mr. SCHANZER. That's why you—the focus on the Palestinian incitement piece of this is important. I mentioned about, you know, this idea of removing—fighting against—once the United States law kicked in I think in 2014 saying that the U.S. will not give money to entities that give money to relatives of suicide bombers.

Some of this money was moved offline through the PLO as opposed to the Palestinian Authority—the Palestinian Liberation Organization, whose income is murky but Abbas is the head of both.

And so there needs to be sure that the signalling is that there's no money to suicide bombers and we're promoting normalization between peoples. The signalling has got to come from the top. I agree with—I think it was Congressman Ros-Lehtinen on that—that there has to be clear signalling.

Now, Abbas has gone on Israeli television in the last couple weeks and said that he's against these knives—these stabbings and it's true that the PA—and this was reported in Defense News—I happened to be sitting with a senior Israeli security official who says it's true—quoting the head of Palestinian intelligence saying that they have disrupted 200 attacks.

They have confiscated knives from the school. They have plainclothesman now at border crossings, you know, to confiscate knives.

So there's a multi-pronged effort here that's needed. There's no silver bullet.

Mr. WEBER. Right. I get that. I just want to make that point, then I want to move on.

I think—back to you, Dr. Schanzer, you also said that the secretary—the Treasury no longer looks at designations for those who are supporting terrorism—that Americans—some of the Muslim are afraid to give to charities because they might—it might be a terroristic charity and some of those charities are civilly liable.

You said something—are there no criminal sanctions in place, laws that say if you give to a terrorist organization contra U.S. laws that you are criminal—you can be charged with a crime?

Mr. SCHANZER. No, sir. We do have an executive order. It's Executive Order 13224. This was the authority that I worked under at the Treasury when I was a terrorism finance analyst and the distinction that I was drawing was that back when I was at Treasury and before we had quite a track record of going after domestic entities that were involved in financing terrorism—so-called charities that were involved in that activity.

Mr. WEBER. But that's criminal, is it not?

Mr. SCHANZER. Well, it's actually under a different order. It's beyond criminal. I mean, it's considered—you know, it's a terrorist act.

Mr. WEBER. And let me just note for the record the judge laid out a whole bunch of organizations that were pretty much anti-Israel but he left out the U.N. I just want to make that distinction.

Let me move on. Dr. Wittes—is that how you say that—you said to stabilize the front line states that have peace treaties with Israel. Who are they and rank them in order.

Ms. WITTES. Rank them in importance?

Mr. WEBER. Yes, ma'am.

Ms. WITTES. I think the most important front line state for Israel is Jordan. It is the bulwark for Israel against the Islamist radicalism of ISIS and other groups to the east, and for a long time it was Israel's land bulwark against an army invasion.

I think that the Jordanian-Israeli peace treaty and the Egyptian-Israeli peace treaty are strong. They are maintained by both sides because they are in both sides——

Mr. WEBER. Okay. I'm out of time, technically. Who are the next ones? Just give me three or four of them.

Ms. WITTES. Well, the only treaties that Israel has with its neighbors are with Jordan and Egypt.

Mr. WEBER. All right. Thank you very much.

Mr. Chairman, thank you. I yield back.

Mr. POE. I thank the gentleman.

I thank all of you all for being here. Without objection, the map that was furnished to you and all the Members of Congress be made a part of the record.

Dr. Schanzer, you made some comments about you would give us information in a different setting. The good lady from Florida made a comment about we will follow up in that because we want that information as well, and Members of Congress may have written questions they will submit to you. We would expect them answered and returned to the Chair.

Thank you all for being here. The subcommittees are adjourned.
[Whereupon, at 3:13 p.m., the hearing was concluded.]

APPENDIX

MATERIAL SUBMITTED FOR THE RECORD

JOINT SUBCOMMITTEE HEARING NOTICE
COMMITTEE ON FOREIGN AFFAIRS
U.S. HOUSE OF REPRESENTATIVES
WASHINGTON, DC 20515-6128

Subcommittee on Terrorism, Nonproliferation, and Trade
Ted Poe (R- TX), Chairman

Subcommittee on the Middle East and North Africa
Ileana Ros-Lehtinen (R-FL), Chairman

TO: MEMBERS OF THE COMMITTEE ON FOREIGN AFFAIRS

You are respectfully requested to attend an OPEN hearing of the Committee on Foreign Affairs, to be held jointly by the Subcommittee on Terrorism, Nonproliferation, and Trade and the Subcommittee on the Middle East and North Africa in Room 2172 of the Rayburn House Office Building (and available live on the Committee website at http://www.ForeignAffairs.house.gov):

DATE: Tuesday, April 19, 2016

TIME: 1:00 p.m.

SUBJECT: Israel Imperiled: Threats to the Jewish State

WITNESSES: Michael Rubin, Ph.D.
                Resident Scholar
                American Enterprise Institute

                Jonathan Schanzer, Ph.D.
                Vice President for Research
                Foundation for Defense of Democracies

                Mr. David Makovsky
                Ziegler Distinguished Fellow
                Irwin Levy Family Program on the U.S.-Israel Strategic Relationship
                The Washington Institute for Near East Policy

                Tamara Cofman Wittes, Ph.D.
                Director
                Center for Middle East Policy
                Brookings Institution

By Direction of the Chairman

COMMITTEE ON FOREIGN AFFAIRS

MINUTES OF SUBCOMMITTEE ON _Terrorism, Nonproliferation, & Trade and the Middle East and North Africa_ HEARING

Day____*Tuesday*____Date____*April 19, 2016*____Room_____*2172*_____

Starting Time ____*1:00 p.m.*____Ending Time ___*3:13 p.m.*___

Recesses |__*1*__| (*1:31 p.m.* to *2:09 p.m.*) (____to ____) (____to ____) (____to ____) (____to ____) (____to ____)

Presiding Member(s)

Chairman Ted Poe

Check all of the following that apply:

Open Session ☑   Electronically Recorded (taped) ☑
Executive (closed) Session ☐   Stenographic Record ☑
Televised ☑

TITLE OF HEARING:

"Israel Imperiled: Threats to the Jewish State"

SUBCOMMITTEE MEMBERS PRESENT:

Reps. Poe, Ros-Lehtinen, Perry, Wilson, Trott, DeSantis, Meadows, Weber, Clawson, Keating, Deutch, Cicilline, Connolly, Kelly, Frankel

NON-SUBCOMMITTEE MEMBERS PRESENT: *(Mark with an * if they are not members of full committee.)*

HEARING WITNESSES: Same as meeting notice attached? Yes ☑ No ☐
(If "no", please list below and include title, agency, department, or organization.)

STATEMENTS FOR THE RECORD: *(List any statements submitted for the record.)*

SFR: submitted by Rep. Connolly

TIME SCHEDULED TO RECONVENE _____
or
TIME ADJOURNED ___*3:13 p.m.*___

Subcommittee Staff Director

Statement for the Record
Submitted by Mr. Connolly of Virginia

Maintenance of the status quo is one of the greatest threats facing Israel today. Besieged on all sides and locked in conflict in perpetuity is not a future we should accept for the United States' closest ally in the Middle East.

Since the Arab-Israeli War of 1948, the security and prosperity of Israel have been hard-fought. While the threats have evolved as the invading armies of five Arab nations have given way to the rockets of Hizballah and Hamas and the myriad threats emanating from their benefactor, Iran, Israel remains adrift in a sea of instability. To the south Israel faces the humanitarian and security crises of Gaza and an ISIL affiliate gaining a foothold in the Sinai Peninsula. To the north, she is greeted with declarations of mass annihilation from the leader of Hizballah, Hassan Nasrallah, and across the Golan Heights, the Syrian war remains unresolved and continues to foster the proliferation of violent extremism.

The United States must take the threats to Israel seriously and deal with them in a credible manner that both ensures Israel's security and calls partners to our shared cause. President Carter's determination throughout thirteen days of negotiations at Camp David wrought the 1979 Egypt-Israel Peace Treaty–a treaty between two countries that were previously in and out of conflict with one another for three decades and which stands to this day. To confront the specter of a nuclear-armed Iran and with the support of the international community, the U.S. led the negotiation of the Joint Comprehensive Plan of Action (JCPOA), which has already verifiably reversed the major components and existing capabilities of the Iranian nuclear program. Both of these diplomatic achievements diminished external threats to Israel's survival and won stakeholders in Israel's security.

Congress has also made serious efforts to confront those who seek to threaten Israel. In December 2015, Congress strengthened economic sanctions on Hizballah with the passage and enactment of the Hizballah International Financing Prevention Act (PL 114-102). Later that month, I joined 6 of my colleagues in writing to the President to request that the Administration take immediate punitive measures in response to Iran's medium-range ballistic missile tests in October and November of 2015. Less than one month later, the President sanctioned 11 individuals and entities for supporting Iran's illicit ballistic missile program. Notably, the sanctions were announced one day after Implementation Day of the JCPOA and demonstrated that the U.S. will both pursue the implementation of the nuclear deal while pressuring Iran for subversive activities outside of the scope of the deal.

Additionally, Congress appropriates substantial bilateral assistance for Israel, totaling $120 billion since 1948. To maintain Israel's Qualitative Military Edge (QME), the current

Administration has provided Israel with more than $20 billion in Foreign Military Financing and $2.9 billion for missile defense programs. This includes more than $1.3 billion for the Iron Dome system, which proved its capability when militants were firing thousands of rockets into Israel from Gaza in the summer of 2014.

In order to further bolster our democratic ally, the U.S. has pursued deepened economic ties with Israel. The U.S.-Israel Free Trade Agreement was the first free trade agreement entered into by the U.S., and bilateral trade with Israel has increased by nearly 600 percent since the pact was signed. The House Foreign Affairs Committee recently marked up and unanimously passed H. Res. 551, recognizing the importance of the U.S.-Israel economic relationship and encouraging new areas of cooperation in energy, water, agriculture, medicine, neurotechnology and cybersecurity.

Turning to the most proximate threat facing Israel, the Israeli-Palestinian conflict remains unresolved more than 20 years after the signing of the Oslo Accords. The most recent surge in violence has claimed the lives of more than 200 Palestinians, 34 Israelis, and two Americans, and both Israeli and Palestinian youth are increasingly disillusioned with the diplomatic path. Just yesterday, a devastating terror attack not unlike those that became common during the second intifada was carried out on a commuter bus.

The U.S. has pursued peace negotiations, blocked one-sided United Nations Security Council Resolutions, condemned Israeli settlements in the West Bank, conditioned aid to the Palestinian authority in order to combat violence, and helped build institutions within Palestinian society that facilitate progress towards a negotiated, two-state solution. There is little hope for credible negotiations without a viable Palestinian negotiating partner or governing authority capable of implementing and safeguarding an ultimate agreement. The wholesale defunding of the Palestinian Authority is a misguided approach to addressing problems with Palestinian governance that undermines an ultimate resolution to the conflict.

Despite the lack of recent progress, the U.S. must continue to be seen as a supporter and independent broker of a lasting peace, and on April 8, I joined with a bipartisan coalition of my colleagues to write the President in support of a continued commitment to the peace process. The U.S. must demonstrate that the peace process is in the interest of Israel's security by rejecting the imposition of a solution on Israel and bolstering the institutions within Palestinian society that facilitate peace negotiations.

A great fear supporters of Israel should have is that 20 years from now the Israeli-Palestinian conflict endures. Whether it is from intransigence, a lack of political will, or honest missteps, it will be our failure and a future generation's price to pay.

www.ingramcontent.com/pod-product-compliance
Lightning Source LLC
Chambersburg PA
CBHW081851280526
45789CB00007B/2652